Study Guide for Zigler and Finn Stevenson's

Children in a Changing World

Development and Social Issues

Alice S. Carter
Yale University

Nancy W. Hall
Yale University

Brooks/Cole Publishing Company
Pacific Grove, California

Brooks/Cole Publishing Company
A Division of Wadsworth, Inc.

Printed in the United States of America

10 9 8 7 6 5 4 3 2 1

ISBN 0-534-14240-0

Sponsoring Editor: Vicki Knight
Editorial Associate: Heather L. Graeve
Production Coordinator: Dorothy Bell
Cover Design: Roy R. Neuhaus
Cover Photo: David Young-Wolff/Photo Edit
Printing and Binding: Malloy Lithographing, Inc.

PREFACE

A Note from the Authors to the Student:

We have prepared this book to help you learn the material presented in Drs. Zigler and Finn-Stevenson's textbook **Children in a Changing World: Development and Social Issues, Second Edition.** The chapters in this study guide are organized in the following manner:

1) Chapter Outline which corresponds directly to the text;
2) Study Goals;
3) Chapter Overview;
4) Key Terms and Concepts;
5) A Matching Exercise;
6) Multiple Choice Self-Test;
7) Recommendations for Further Reading;
8) Answer Key for Self-Test Items.

This study guide is not intended to replace the textbook. In studying, you may find it most helpful to first read the chapter in the text, then to review the study goals and chapter overview presented in the study guide. Finally, check your grasp of the material by completing the key terms, matching, and multiple choice exercises at the end of each chapter in the study guide. Recommendations for further reading include popular works related to the chapter, up-to-date research reports, and classic books and articles related to the chapter content.

Child Observations:

In our experience, students benefit most from courses on child development when they have the opportunity to integrate materials from readings and lectures with observations of children working and playing in their natural settings (e.g, playgrounds, schools, daycare centers, home, grocery stores, churches and synagogues). Once you begin to look, you will see children everywhere! Babysitting often provides an opportunity for closer observations. Students often find it useful to apply some of the more structured observational methods presented in Chapter 2. For example, two students in the class might develop their own behavior coding system. This involves deciding on the behaviors which will be observed (e.g., hitting, smiling, cooperation) and

developing a coding sheet to rate behaviors. Observing a
child jointly can lead to discussions and a deeper
understanding of issues such as reliability and observer
bias.

Public Policy:

As you take this course, you will be exposed to legal and
political issues that affect children and families.
Monitoring newspaper reports about legislation,
educational policies, and advocacy groups can provide
excellent examples of ways in which larger social issues
influence the lives of children and families. As one
goal of this course is to sensitize you to child and
family social policy issues, monitoring newspaper
accounts will inform you about activities in your own
community and help you to recognize how the study of
child development is applicable to everyday life.

Many hands contributed to the preparation of this volume.
The authors gratefully acknowledge the patience and help
of Cynthia Kelly, Karen Sampara, Melissa Schmidt, and
Claire Timme, and the helpful advice of Matia Finn
Stevenson and Edward Zigler at Yale, and of Vicki Knight
at Brooks/Cole. On the home fronts, this volume could
not have been completed without the patience,
forbearance, and support of Gary, Rachel, and Zack
Carter, and David and Wilson Howell.

Alice S. Carter

Nancy W. Hall

CONTENTS

CHAPTER 1

CHILDREN AND SOCIAL CHANGE

STUDY GOALS

After studying Chapter 1, you should have a good grasp of the following ideas and trends.

1.   The reasons for studying child development and the changes in the reasons over the past decades.

2.   The identities and contributions of major figures in the history of child and adolescent psychology, not merely as historical figures, but as thinkers whose work and ideas are reflected in modern psychological thought.

3.   How the study of child development is influenced by social, demographic, and technological changes. How such changes pose challenges for developmental psychology and how these challenges are met.

4.   The roles of support programs and child advocates in implementing positive changes for children and families.

CHAPTER OVERVIEW

Chapter 1 introduces the reader to the field of child development and some of early contributors to the field and presents significant historical contributions. Next, several current research trends are explored to illustrate the role of child development research in promoting social change. The chapter places a special emphasis on elucidating the centrality of social policy in the field of child development.

Why Study Children?

a.   To understand better the nature of adults;
b.   To understand better ways to enhance development, thereby improving the lives of children.

John Locke: (1632-1704) -- English

    a. believed that the child was an incomplete adult who was governed by urges and desires which must be controlled through structuring the environment;
    b. viewed child's mind at birth as a "tabula rasa";
    c. stated that the goal of education is to enhance the child's self-discipline and self-control.

Jean-Jacques Rousseau: (1712-1778) -- French

    a. viewed the child as a "noble savage" who possesses an intuitive knowledge of right and wrong;
    b. stated that the goal of education is to provide opportunities for exploration and learning.

Charles Darwin: (1809-1882) -- English

    a. set forth the principles of natural selection and evolution thereby focusing scientists' interest on the development of human beings.
    b. created one of the first baby biographies (see below).

Early Observational and Empirical Studies:

    Baby Biographies. Day to day accounts of children's development, or written observations maintained in baby biographies, was the first method used to study children's development.

G. Stanley Hall (1846-1924) and Early Experimental Studies:

    G. Stanley Hall founded the American Psychological Association and is credited as the founder of child and adolescent psychology as subareas of general psychology. Hall collected information in a systematic manner, often using questionnaires, from a large number of child subjects in order to make generalizations about child and adolescent development.

Why Focus on Social Policy?

    An assumption is made that research should be directed toward the solution of contemporary social problems.

<u>Childhood Social Indicators</u>. Measures of changes or constancies in the conditions of children's lives (e.g., infant mortality, child abuse rates, number of children in poverty, rates of mental health disorders).

Growing Up in the 1990s:

A number of changes and transformations have occurred in family structure and the roles and responsibilities which family members assume. These changes have made the task of childrearing more complex than in the past, often creating stressful conditions for children and parents. Among the contributing factors are:

1. Fragmentation and isolation of the family as evidenced by the growth in single parent households which increase children's risk for living in conditions of poverty and the increase in moving long distances to pursue employment which disrupts kin and long term social-support relationships; and

2. **Poverty** is a reality for an increasing number of American families -- especially families with young children and black and Hispanic families. The ramifications of living in poverty are numerous and include assaults on children's physical, cognitive and emotional health. Some of these effects are due to increased risk associated with exposure to environmental stressors and feelings of powerlessness and frustration which often are experienced by the poor.

Social policy has not kept pace with the dramatic changes in American life. However, research in child development has 1) brought attention to the fact that many children are living in conditions that are potentially damaging to their development, altering our perceptions of the problems society is facing, and 2) had a profound impact on family life, by presenting information which is used to shape the social policies which lead to major societal changes.

Working Mothers:

Full-time employment for women with school-aged children has been relatively common for about two decades

3

with upward of 70 percent of women now working out of the home. Only recently, however, has there been a dramatic increase in the numbers of women with infants and preschool children working outside of the home and among these a significant percentage are returning to work very shortly after giving birth. Research findings suggest that maternal employment per se is not deleterious to child development. It is the stress associated with fulfilling multiple roles and concerns about the unavailability of adequate child care while working. Social policy efforts are directed toward decreasing the stress associated with the dual roles of working and parenting and toward increasing the availability of quality child care.

Divorce:

The number of divorces per year seems to have reached its peak and is leveling off. Nonetheless, 40-50 percent of U.S. children will experience the divorce of their parents. Research on the children of divorce suggests that divorce is not a unitary event for children but a series of stressful transitions. In addition to the many stages of family reorganization which follow divorce, more and more children are experiencing the remarriage of one or both parents, resulting in **stepfamilies**. One particularly stressful event for children is involvement in a custody or **legal battle for the child**.

Changes in Demography:

The composition of our population has changed dramatically with the unusually high birth rates of the two decades after World War II (baby boom), the decline in birth rate we are now experiencing (which is in part associated with an overwhelming trend for later marriage and childbearing), and increased longevity. Ours has become an aging society.

Learning from Other Cultures: Population Policies in China. A **natural experiment** was undertaken in China in an effort to contain the population growth which was reaching crisis proportions. A vigorous government program combines persuasion with economic incentives and penalties aimed at achieving one-child families. Research to date indicates that children in one-child

4

families evidence superior intellectual abilities but also display a higher incidence of many negative social behaviors.

Technological Advances:

Growing up with TV and computers presents many opportunities for children, but this technology has also changed the way children are growing up, what they are exposed to and at what age, and the way that children are taught. Estimates of children's television watching vary considerably, but there is agreement that American children spend more time watching TV than in any other activity. Several studies have documented a link between violence on television and aggressive behavior in children. Children are extremely attentive to commercials and may be especially vulnerable to the media's attempt to develop an attitude of **"continuous consumption."** Several advocacy groups are especially concerned about the media's special efforts to target children as consumers (e.g., by increasing the rate of commercials during peak child viewing hours). TV viewing also decreases **family interaction** -- the amount of time families spend actively interacting with one another (e.g., talking, playing games, etc.). TV can be used as a learning tool as evidenced by slow-action shows which encourage viewer involvement and introduce social skills (e.g., Mr. Rogers). In contrast to TV viewing, which is essentially a passive activity, reading is an active activity which allows a person to reflect and create a series of images, thereby challenging our mental skills and enhancing our imagination.

From Problem to Solution: Addressing the Needs of Children:

Family Support Programs is a term used to describe a wide range of programs which share a goal of helping to strengthen families by providing emotional, informational, and instrumental assistance, thus enabling individuals to cope with the stressors of family life. While these programs vary in terms of services rendered and populations served they all address the family as a unit in contrast to a focus on the child in isolation.

The Role of Government:

The government can support all families by enacting laws pertaining to child care and parental leave. Government support is especially significant in the case of poor families. Aid to Families with Dependent Children (AFDC) provides support (e.g., food stamps and health care) to families living below the poverty level. In 1988 the U.S. Congress enacted the Family Support Act. This law calls for stronger work, education, and training requirements for those receiving AFDC assistance.

The Integration of Child Development Research and Social Policy:

We can base government policies facilitating family life on social indicators, thus guiding policy development.

The principle of integrity and continuity states that children and families benefit if the integrity and continuity of the family are maintained. Despite general acceptance of this principle, our foster care program often serves to break up families by moving children in a manner which discourages emotional attachments.

The Role of Business and Industry:

In view of dwindling government funds, we must look beyond the public sector to the private sector for support for children and families. The interdependence of work and family life is beginning to be reflected in changes in the work structure which allow flexible work arrangements, part-time job opportunities, more liberal maternity leave policies and on-site child care centers. In an attempt to increase the number of child care facilities, several cities use zoning regulations to ensure that businesses help with child care.

The Role of Schools:

Many schools have begun to implement programs that teach interpersonal or social problem-solving in addition to the traditional academic courseload. **The School of the 21st Century** provides an integrated site for offering extra-academic programs for students along with family support and child care. The major components include resource and referral services to help parents find care for infants and toddlers, all-day care for preschoolers, and before- and after-school and vacation care for children from kindergarten through age 12. Home visitation involving parent education is available for families with children ages birth to three as well as a network of educational and support services for family day care providers in the community.

The Role of Advocates:

Changes in the way that government, industry, or the schools operate cannot occur in the absence of **advocacy** -- a combination of acting in behalf of one's own interests, pleading the cause of others, and defending or maintaining a cause. Child advocates are involved in monitoring the conditions of children's lives and attempting to change the systems which can provide for their needs through education and recommendations for reform.

KEY TERMS AND CONCEPTS

Complete the following sentences with the most appropriate word or phrase. Check your responses against the correct answers at the end of the chapter.

1. John Locke compared the human newborn to a
_____.

2. Rousseau conceptualized the child as a
_____.

3. Darwin's work emphasized _____ among species.

4. _____ are indices of change in the conditions of children's lives.

5. Children in self care are known as _____ children.

6. _____ families is a new term for stepfamilies.

7. The _____ following World War II brought unusually high birth rates for two decades.

8. In _____ scientists take advantage of naturally occurring events to study the effects of social change.

9. _____ efforts differ from traditional interventions because they do not focus on the child in isolation.

10. Promotion of awareness of and solutions for the problems of children and families comes under the broad general heading of _____.

MATCHING EXERCISES

Test your knowledge of the important people discussed in Chapter 1. Answers appear at the end of this chapter.

1. John Locke   a. father of American child study

2. Jean-Jacques Rousseau   b. standardized testing

3. Charles Darwin   c. child as a noble savage

4. G. Stanley Hall   d. tabula rasa

5. Alfred Binet   e. continuity among species

MULTIPLE CHOICE SELF-TEST

Answers appear at the end of this chapter.

_____1. Family support programs
a. support only the parents, not the child
b. are often informal, grass roots programs
c. are usually heavily subsidized by the government
d. are not as effective as programs which only treat the child

_____2. What percentage of mothers of infants under one work outside the home?
a. 70
b. 20
c. 94
d. 97

_____3. Roughly what percentage of children under 18 have a diagnosable mental illness?
a. 3%
b. 12%
c. 50%
d. 87%

_____4. Children's adjustment to divorce is affected by
a. age
b. sex
c. birth order
d. all of the above

_____5. The Father of American Psychology was
a. B. F. Skinner
b. Sigmund Freud
c. G. Stanley Hall
d. Benjamin Spock

_____6. Divorce affects about _____ of all U.S. children.
a. 1/10
b. half
c. 90%
d. 99%

_____7. The work of Goldstein, Freud, and Solnit focused on
a. dream analysis for small children
b. how to curb rising divorce rates
c. how to become a child advocate
d. protecting the child's interests in legal battles

_____8. The credit for the use and development of the questionnaire as a research tool in psychology goes to
a. Sigmund Freud
b. Anna Freud
c. Jean-Jacques Rousseau
d. G. Stanley Hall

_____9. The characterization of the human infant as a blank slate, or _tabula_ _rasa_, was a feature of _____'s work.
a. John Locke
b. Al Solnit
c. Jean-Jacques Rousseau
d. G. Stanley Hall

_____10. Poverty and childhood mental health disorders are
a. negatively correlated
b. positively correlated
c. completely unrelated
d. mutually exclusive

SUGGESTIONS FOR FURTHER READING

Anderson, J. F. (1956). Child development: An historical perspective. Child Development, 27, 181-197.

Aries, P. (1962). Centuries of Childhood: A Social History of Family Life. New York: Alfred A. Knopf.

Borstelman, L. J. (1983). Children before psychology: Ideas about children from antiquity to the late 1800s. In W. Kessen (Ed.), Handbook of Child Psychology, Vol. 1: History, theory and methods (pp. 1-40). New York: John Wiley and Sons.

Greenleaf, B. K. (1978). Children Through the Ages: A History of Childhood. New York: McGraw-Hill.

Kessen, W. (1965). The Child. New York: John Wiley and Sons.

Konner, M. (1991). Childhood. New York: Little, Brown & Company.

Ross, D. G. (1972). G. Stanley Hall: The Psychologist as Prophet. Chicago: University of Chicago Press.

Senn, M. J. E. (1975). Insights on the child development movement in the United States. Monographs of the Society for Research in Child Development, 40 (3-4, Serial No. 161).

ANSWER KEY FOR SELF-TEST ITEMS

Key Terms and Concepts

1.	<u>tabula</u> <u>rasa</u>	6.	reconstituted
2.	noble savage	7.	baby boom
3.	continuity	8.	natural experiments
4.	childhood social indicators	9.	family support
5.	latchkey	10.	advocacy

Matching

1-d, 2-c, 3-e, 4-a, 5-b

Multiple Choice

1.	b	6.	b
2.	a	7.	d
3.	b	8.	d
4.	d	9.	a
5.	c	10.	b

CHAPTER 2

THE STUDY OF CHILD DEVELOPMENT

STUDY GOALS

After reviewing Chapter 2, you should be able to explain the following:

1. Major events and figures in the history of child study from the 19th century to the present, and how their contributions are reflected in the ways we study and treat children today.

2. What a theory is, what determines its usefulness, the major theoretical perspectives guiding child study today, and how they are alike and different from each other.

3. The differences among various types and methods of research, and which types are applicable to which situations.

4. What ethical principles must be observed when conducting research involving children and families, and what issues arise out of the application of these principles.

CHAPTER OVERVIEW

HISTORICAL HIGHLIGHTS

The Testing Movement:

Alfred Binet, a psychologist, and **Theodore Simon**, a physician, developed an intelligence test in 1905 in response to a request of the Ministry of Public Education in France. Its purpose was to distinguish between children of normal intelligence and subnormal intelligence so that children could be placed in appropriate educational settings. This test was translated and refined for use in America by **Lewis Terman** (the Stanford-Binet). The test, scored in terms of IQ, or **intelligence quotient**

(the ratio of a child's mental age to chronological age), was a powerful predictor of children's performance in school.

Increased Popularity of Child Study:

Arnold Gesell (1880-1961) emphasized the role of maturational mechanisms in development (and minimized the role of environment) based on his observations and documentation of full-term, preterm, and impaired infants. He developed age standards for development in motor, visual, language, and social behavior. He argued that certain **orderly stages of development** formed a **universal** and **invariant sequence.** This began the era in which many child study centers and laboratory schools were established in universities to learn more about children's development and to use this understanding to facilitate child rearing, education and teacher training. While the early part of the 1900's was characterized by the accumulation of large stores of descriptive data, by the middle of the century researchers became less interested in generating data and turned their attention to the testing of developmental theories.

THEORIES IN CHILD DEVELOPMENT

What Is a Theory?

A **theory** is a statement or set of statements offered to explain a phenomenon. It is also a way of organizing ideas and empirical information. A theory often provides directions for future research.

Testability:

Scientific theories are governed by a set of rules which include **testability,** that **hypotheses** (specific predictions derived from the theory) can be supported by observable events.

Major Theories in Child Development:

Theories of development can be divided into several categories:

epigenetic theories, which explain development and

behavior on the basis of the interaction between the environment and a person's genetic inheritance; and **environmental theories**, which explain behavior on the basis of an individual's past experience and learning. In addition, there are variations in the scope of the theory and the aspect of development addressed (e.g., cognition, emotion). Adopting a different theoretical perspective can lead to markedly discrepant interpretations of development.

To date, no one theory is sufficient.

The Psychoanalytic Theory. Sigmund Freud (1856-1939) developed the **psychoanalytic theory**, a biological theory of personality, in Vienna. A physician and neurologist by training, Freud was influenced by Josef Breuer, who was treating patients with hypnosis. Freud later developed the technique of free association which was used instead of hypnosis to uncover events or conflicts which were repressed in **unconscious** memory. Freud divided human personality functioning into the **id**, characterized by biological instinctual energy, the **ego**, which psychologically regulates the balance between reality constraints and primitive desires, and the **superego**, which represents social and societal values and traditions. Freud also discussed psychosexual stages in development, organized by the focus of the id (oral zone, anal zone, phallic zone, latency period, and genital period). Failure to resolve a conflict at a given stage led to **fixation**, and resulted in personality problems.

The Psychosocial Theory. **Erik Erikson** (1903-   ) developed a psychosocial theory which emphasized emotional development and highlighted the role of social demands. Erikson stated that conflicts and psychological difficulties could develop at any stage of life, including adulthood and old age, if the individual failed to resolve specific crises associated with their stage of development. Erikson's stages are: **trust vs. mistrust** during infancy; **autonomy vs. shame** in toddlerhood; **initiative vs. guilt** in the preschool years; **industry vs. inferiority** in the school aged years; **identity vs. role confusion** in adolescence; **intimacy vs. isolation** in early adulthood; **generativity vs. stagnation** in middle adulthood; and **ego integrity vs. despair** in old age.

Learning Theory. **Behaviorism**, or **traditional learning theory**, is concerned with those behaviors which can be observed and measured. Behaviorists believe that human beings advance in their development through learning. At the extreme of this view, **John Watson** argued that the child is a blank slate waiting to be trained. Watson advocated treating children as though they were young adults (1928).

There are two kinds of conditioning: classical and operant. In **classical conditioning** or respondent conditioning, responses under involuntary control become learned reactions to environmental events through association. In **operant conditioning**, the organism operates on the environment to produce a change that will lead to a reward. As described by **B. F. Skinner**, the principles of reward and punishment are employed to shape or modify behavior.

Social Learning Theory. An outgrowth of learning theory, classical and operant principles are employed along with vicarious learning or modeling to explain aspects of social behavior. The child is viewed as an active agent and the role of reciprocal relationships among cognition, environmental factors, and behavior is acknowledged.

Theories of Cognitive Development. **Cognition** refers to the way in which we gain knowledge, or construct our experience, through perception, memory, and thought processing. Development is viewed as undergoing a series of reorganizations rather than a process of cumulative change.

Piaget's theory and information processing theory have dominated the field of cognitive research. **Jean Piaget** (1896-1980) referred to his work as **genetic epistemology**. **Epistemology** is the study of the nature of knowledge. Piaget argued that all knowledge comes from action and that the individual is active in acquiring knowledge. In addition, Piaget argued that children's ability to reason, which is associated with underlying **cognitive structures**, differs according to their developmental stage. These stages, which unfold in a constant order, are: **sensorimotor** (0-2 years); **preoperational** (2-7 years); **concrete operational** (7-12 years); and **formal operational thinking** (12-).

Heinz Werner (1890-1964) proposed the **orthogenetic principle,** which specifies that development proceeds from a global, undifferentiated state to one of higher differentiation and integration. This is in part accomplished through the process of **hierarchic integration,** in which behavioral responses and skills are increasingly organized into hierarchies. Werner stressed that human development is marked by both change and stability; people go through an ordered sequence of developmental stages which allow different ways of understanding the environment. Each stage is characterized by **adaptive change** and **organizational stability.**

The Information-Processing Approach. Information processing subsumes many theories of cognition which share certain assumptions. First, the mind is viewed as a system for storing and retrieving information. Second, individuals actively process and transform information from the environment. Finally, the limits of an individual's capacity to process information are acknowledged.

SOURCES OF IDEAS AND EVIDENCE

The Cross-Cultural Approach:

Psychologists and anthropologists who study children in different cultures have refined our understanding of how children learn to behave in ways that are acceptable in different cultures. This method of study highlights aspects of development which appear primarily driven by innate determinants, or maturation (e.g., aspects of language progression), and which appear to be influenced by culture (i.e., environment and experience).

The cross-cultural approach has been employed by anthropologists and psychologists to study minority group children in the United States. Turning away from a model which views differences in minority group practices as deficiencies, researchers such as John Ogbu attempt to examine differences within their cultural contexts.

The Behavioral-Genetic Approach:

This approach seeks to examine the extent to which

17

genes contribute to the development of behavioral traits. More recently, complex models which attempt to account for the influences of genes and environment at multiple points in development are studied.

The Comparative Approach:

This approach examines an aspect of human behavior in relation to similar behaviors in other species. Harry Harlow's work on separation and attachment with rhesus monkeys is an excellent example.

The Ethological Approach:

Closely related to the comparative approach, the ethological approach focuses on the evolutionary origins of behavior with an emphasis on behaviors occurring in the natural environment. Research on **imprinting**, a process responsible for attachment during a critical period of development, is paradigmatic of this approach. John Bowlby applied this approach to the study of infants, noting that there are **species-typical behaviors** that help them maintain proximity to their mothers and that this proximity has evolutionary value in terms of increased probability of survival.

The Ecological Approach:

The ecological approach refers to the study of the organism in its natural environment.

DIMENSIONS OF CHILD DEVELOPMENT RESEARCH

Research Evidence and Personal Knowledge:

Hypotheses which are derived from theory or earlier empirical studies are tested through research. By describing methods in great detail, knowledge derived from research can be scrutinized by other investigators. Types of Research: Applied and Basic:

The term **applied research** defines any research which is designed to meet society's needs or to provide information that can be put to immediate use. **Basic research**, on the other hand, is not motivated by a social need but by the desire to expand human knowledge.

18

Methods for Research with Children:

Normative studies provide information about the sequence and "average age" of the appearance of capacities. The **observational method** requires researchers to collect information as they watch (or videotape) and record their behavior. To ensure accuracy, researchers assess inter-rater reliability, or the extent to which two observers code the same information. Validity refers to both the behavior under study and the **representativeness** of the sample of subjects under study. In the **experimental method** the researcher attempts to examine the effect of **independent variables**, which are manipulated, on the **dependent variable(s)**. In an experiment, subjects are **randomly assigned** to levels of the independent variable. In **field experiments** research is conducted in the natural setting. The independent variable is still manipulated or deliberately changed to evaluate the effect of the change on the dependent variable(s). In **natural experiments**, a change which is not due to a research intervention occurs and is evaluated. The **correlational method** assesses the degree of association between two variables. The two most common kinds of correlational relationships are **positive relationships** (as one increases the other increases) and **negative relationships** (as one increases the other decreases). Tests of **statistical significance** are employed to determine whether or not an association between variables is greater than would occur by chance. **Longitudinal studies**, which can involve correlational or experimental methods, enable researchers to study changes (stability and instability) in an individuals's behavior over time. Problems associated with longitudinal research involve: cost, subject attrition, practice effects following repeat testing, and historical events. **Cross-sectional studies** are often employed to overcome some of the disadvantages of longitudinal studies while examining developmental questions by comparing groups of subjects at different age levels rather than by following the same individuals over time. A central problem associated with cross-sectional studies is the influence of **cohort effects**, or exposure of different age groups to differing experiences. Researchers often use a **combined longitudinal and cross-sectional approach**, following several groups of children at different ages for a shorter period of time. **Retrospective research** involves asking questions about earlier events in an individual's life. **Case histories** involve the in depth study of a single individual.

Ethical Considerations:

The Society for Research in Child Development has established the following ethical standards for research with children:

1. Each child must be fully informed about the purposes of the study and the procedures to be employed; if the child is too young, parental consent must be obtained;
2. Each child or parent may withdraw at any time during the study;
3. Children will not be subjected to harmful treatment during the study;
4. All information about individual participants will be kept confidential;
5. No matter how young the child he or she has rights that supersede the investigator's rights.

While these guidelines are clear, sometimes ethical dilemmas are present in research with children and their families.

KEY TERMS AND CONCEPTS

Check your answers against those at the end of this chapter.

1. The _____ is the ratio of mental age to chronological age.

2. The idea of _____ readiness was central to Gesell's work.

3. The experimental variable controlled by the experimenter is the _____ variable.

4. The outcome variable is the _____ variable.

5. Studies which follow one group of subjects to assess change over time are called _____ studies.

6. Studies which take advantage of social events which are not set up by the researcher are _____ experiments.

7. The first stage of cognitive development in Piaget's theory is the _____.

8. Gesell concluded that developmental stages occur in _____ sequence.

9. The theories of Locke and Rousseau differed, but both emphasized the role of _____ in child development.

10. By contrast, the theories of Gesell and Vygotsky rely heavily upon the concept of _____.

MATCHING EXERCISE

1. Arnold Gesell
2. Sigmund Freud
3. Erik Erikson
4. John B. Watson
5. B. F. Skinner
6. Jean Piaget
7. Heinz Werner
8. Lev Vygotsky
9. Margaret Mead
10. Harry Harlow
11. John Bowlby
12. Urie Bronfenbrenner

a. stages of psychosexual development
b. founded Yale Child Study Center
c. traditional learning theory
d. zone of proximal development
e. progressive resolution of conflicts
f. operant conditioning
g. ecological approach
h. orthogenetic principles
i. cross-cultural pioneer
j. species-typical behavior
k. genetic epistemology
l. comparative attachment research

MULTIPLE CHOICE SELF-TEST

Answers appear at the end of this chapter.

_____1. How are the theories of Locke and Rousseau similar?
a. both stressed the importance of heredity
b. both believed the child was born with certain innate concepts
c. both stressed the influence of experience on development
d. both played an important role in the development of traditional learning theory

_____ 2. Which of these is not a Piagetian cognitive stage?
a. preoperational
b. formal operational
c. sensorimotor
d. oral

_____ 3. The intelligence quotient is defined as
a. the number of items correctly answered on the Stanford-Binet
b. the child's mental age
c. the child's mental age X 100
d. the ratio of mental age to chronological age

_____ 4. The core of Erikson's developmental theory is
a. moving past the Oedipal conflict
b. resolution of particular crises at each stage of development
c. the distinction between operant and classical conditioning
d. the child's ability to use different reasoning strategies at different ages

_____ 5. G. Stanley Hall's greatest contribution to child study was
a. the founding of the Yale Child Study Center
b. his diary of observations of his son's behavior
c. the promotion of empirical research
d. founding the Society for Research in Child Development

_____ 6. Which of these is not a stage of psychosexual development, according to psychoanalytic theory?
a. oral
b. anal
c. sensorimotor
d. genital

_____ 7. The label "the terrible twos" was coined by
a. Freud
b. Gesell
c. Binet
d. Spock

_____8. Harold Skeels' work had implications for our understanding of
   a. the impact of the environment on cognitive development
   b. classical conditioning
   c. IQ testing
   d. mother-infant bonding

_____9. In a study of the effects of day care on IQ, the amount of time spent in day care would be
   a. an extraneous variable
   b. an experimental confound
   c. a dependent variable
   d. an independent variable

_____10. Child study was popularized in the U.S. in
   a. the mid-18th century
   b. the 1930s and 1940s
   c. the late 1980s
   d. the late 19th century

RECOMMENDATIONS FOR FURTHER READING

Appignanesi, R. (1979). Freud for Beginners. New York: Pantheon Books.

Cairns, R. B. (1983). The emergence of developmental psychology. In W. Kessen (Ed.), Handbook of Child Psychology. Vol. 1: History, Theory, and Methods (pp. 41-102). New York: John Wiley and Sons.

Gay, P. (1988). Freud: A Life for Our Time. New York: W. W. Norton & Company.

Gould, J. (1981). The Mismeasure of Man. New York: W. W. Norton & Company.

Piaget, J. (1977). The Essential Piaget. New York: Basic Books.

Siegel, L. S. (1991). On the maturation of developmental psychology. In F. S. Kessel, M. H. Bornstein, & A. J. Sameroff (Eds.), Contemporary Constructions of the Child: Essays in Honor of William Kessen. Hillsdale, NJ: Lawrence Erlbaum Associates, Publishers.

Smuts, A. B., & Hagen, J. W. (1985). History and research in child development. Monographs of the Society for Research in Child Development, 50 (4-5, Serial No. 211).

ANSWER KEY FOR SELF-TEST ITEMS

Key Terms and Concepts

1.	intelligence quotient	6.	naturalistic
2.	maturational	7.	preoperational
3.	independent	8.	invariant
4.	dependent	9.	experience
5.	longitudinal	10.	maturation

Matching

1-b, 2-a, 3-e, 4-c, 5-f, 6-k, 7-h, 8-d, 9-i,

10-l, 11-j, 12-g

Multiple Choice

1.	c	5.	c	9.	d
2.	d	6.	c	10.	b
3.	d	7.	b		
4.	b	8.	a		

CHAPTER 3

OUR BIOLOGICAL HERITAGE

STUDY GOALS

After reading Chapter 3, you should have a clear understanding of the following constructs:

1. The mechanics of genetic transmission of traits and diseases, including an understanding of cell structure and division, Mendel's laws, complex gene activity, and genetic variability.

2. Gene-environment transactions, including specific examples thereof.

3. The practical applications of genetics, including prediction of medical anomalies, genetic screening, and genetic counseling.

4. The social policy aspect of genetic research, including an awareness of the implications of our growing ability to manipulate our biological heritage for policy, law, and medical and research ethics.

CHAPTER OVERVIEW

GENE-ENVIRONMENT TRANSACTIONS

Human development is the result of complex transactions between genetic and environmental factors. An appreciation of the role of genetic factors in development and the specific mechanisms of genetic transmission is crucial for understanding individual variation.

A **genotype** is the genetic makeup of the individual. A **phenotype** is the individual's observable and/or measurable characteristic. A given genotype may give rise to many phenotypes depending on the environments that genotype encounters through development. The possible phenotypes are not limitless; rather boundaries are set by the genotype (i.e., **range of reaction**). The genetic endowment a child is born with should be viewed as an individual's potential. The extent to which it is realized depends on environmental experiences and a complex transaction between genetic and environmental factors. In the **Transactional Model of Development** proposed by Sameroff and Chandler (1975), the reciprocal influences of phenotype and environment are described. For example, a baby who is irritable due to a genetic predisposition may contribute to environmental experiences (i.e., the parenting methods employed) which will either exacerbate or minimize the baby's predisposition toward irritability. Finally, the notion of **critical periods** refers to the timing of environmental experiences (e.g., a fetus may be especially vulnerable to certain drugs in the intrauterine environment during the first trimester of the pregnancy, resulting in physical or behavioral abnormalities).

Canalization (or preparedness) refers to the existence of some characteristics which are very difficult to modify and thus are acquired in a wide range of environments.

Gregor Mendel (1822-1884) -- "The father of modern genetics." By studying peas, Mendel developed several principles or laws of inheritance. At any given gene locus there are two **alleles**, an alternative form of the gene. A child is said to be **homozygous** for a trait when two alleles contain the same hereditary direction for the determination of the trait (AA). A child is said to be **heterozygous** when the alleles are different (Aa). Alleles behave in a pattern of **dominance** (where the presence of one allele determines the phenotype -- A?) and **recessiveness** (where the absence of the dominant allele determines the phenotype -- aa). Many disorders, some of which are life-threatening, are passed on to offspring by parents who both have the recessive allele for a particular condition (e.g., albinism, phenylketonuria or PKU). PKU, a condition which causes mental retardation, is treatable through dietary therapy. A treated PKU infant, who develops normal intellectual functioning, is a **phenocopy**, or an individual whose phenotype mimics the phenotype usually associated with another specific genotype. The phenocopy individual appears and functions normally, but their genotype has not been changed. Thus, in the case of PKU, the phenocopy individual will transmit the recessive gene associated with PKU. The reverse side of the phenocopy

27

PKU phenomenon is that a woman with PKU who has escaped brain damage may carry a heterozygous (genetically unaffected) child if she marries a person who transmits the dominant allele. However, if the woman is untreated, she will have a high concentration of toxic substances in her uterus which will harm her unborn child and cause brain damage.

Modes of Inheritance:

Up until now, we have been reviewing **single-gene** heredity patterns. Often a number of genes may be involved in the expression of a single trait. This phenomenon is called **polygenetic inheritance**. In a separate phenomenon, **pleiotropy**, single genes can influence more than one trait. **Modifier genes** influence the actions or observable characteristics of other genes.

Chemical Nature of Genes:

Genes function in the cellular environment. While most cells have specialized functions (e.g., brain cells vs. heart cells), all cells have similar, basic component parts: 1) An outer membrane, or **cell wall**; 2) fluid, called the **cytoplasm**; and 3) a compact structure floating in the center called the nucleus. **Deoxyribonucleic acid**, or **DNA**, is the genetic material which is located in the nucleus on long tiny fibers called **chromatin**. DNA contains a genetic code which is used to direct the operational functioning of **ribonucleic acid**, or **RNA**. RNA serves as a messenger to bring instructions from the nucleus of a cell to its cytoplasm, where the instructions are carried out. A section of the code is called a gene. Human beings have 46 chromosomes in each cell. Each chromosome holds thousands of genes. Genetic information is coded by the ordering of the chemical steps at different locations on the chromosome.

Beginning of Fetal Development and Cell Division:

The **zygote** is formed when a **sperm cell** from the father penetrates and fuses with the **ovum cell** (the egg) from the mother. The sperm cell and ovum cell are termed **gametes**, or reproductive cells. All other cells, which comprise various body elements, are called **somatic**, or body cells. Gametes have 23 chromosomes each. Somatic cells have 23 pairs of chromosomes, or 46 chromosomes.

The cells of the zygote multiply rapidly by **mitosis**, the process of somatic cells dividing. Gametes are formed by **meiosis**. Some genetic variability is a function of **crossing over**, a process which occurs during meiosis involving an exchange of genes between pairs of chromosomes. Genetic variation can also result from mutation, which are changes in a gene, in the arrangements of genes on a chromosome or in the quantity of chromosomal material. **Down syndrome**, occurring in 1 of 500 births, is caused by a mutation, translocation, or nondisjunction on chromosome 21. In **translocation** part of the chromosome attaches itself to another chromosome. **Nondisjunction** is the failure of a chromosome to separate during meiosis in the egg.

Each cell nucleus contains 22 autosomes and 1 sex chromosome, in males XY and in females XX. Fathers determine the sex of the offspring as they can contribute either an X or a Y; thus the zygote has a fifty-fifty chance of being XY or XX, that is, male or female. Sex-linked disorders occur because some recessive genes on the X chromosome have no matching allele on the Y chromosome to counteract its effect (e.g., hemophilia). Occasionally, gametes form which have an abnormal number of chromosomes. One such condition affecting females is **Turner's syndrome**, in which there is an absence of the sex chromosome X (XO instead of XX) and several specific physical abnormalities. A condition affecting males is **Klinefelter syndrome**, in which the affected individual has an extra X chromosome (XXY instead of XY). We can see these abnormalities using a **karyotype**, an edited photographic arrangement of chromosomes.

The Gene Advantage and Natural Selection:

Evolution is the process of a species' changing over time. Natural selection refers to the process whereby organisms who are better adapted to a given environment will be more likely to reproduce and survive. A high frequency of a gene may be maintained in a population in a given environment when the homozygous recessive condition results in affected status but the heterozygous genotype confers protection from the specific environment (e.g., sickle cell - malaria). Ethnic origin influences the likelihood of carrying the genotype for specific disorders.

In **genetic counseling** couples can be informed about the probability of their having a child with various disorders given either knowledge of the parents' genotypes or carefully evaluated family history information. **Genetic screening** can be done prenatally or postnatally to identify risk for particular diseases. The newest such test, conducted in the ninth week of pregnancy, is the **chorion biopsy**. It involves taking a sample of the chorion, the outer member of the amniotic sac, which contains the same genetic material as the embryo. The results can be obtained within a few days of the exam. However, in approximately 1 percent of cases the test can lead to spontaneous abortion. Amniocentesis, which involves taking a sample of the amniotic fluid, can be conducted after the tenth week of pregnancy. The results are known in three weeks. It may lead to pressure changes in the fetal ear that result in abnormalities in anatomical development. A third prenatal test, **alpha-fetoprotein screening**, involves drawing blood from the pregnant woman to determine whether or not the fetus is suffering from neural tube defects which result in mental retardation. Abnormalities can also be detected with a **sonogram**, which gives a detailed picture of the fetus through high frequency sound waves. Finally, a recently developed procedure to detect the fetus's sex involves an analysis of the mother's blood, which contains fetal cells. If there are Y chromosomes in the blood the fetus is male. Ethical issues are raised in the use of such tests due to both the risk to the fetus and the possibility of terminating the pregnancy based on the information obtained in the prenatal testing. Other ethical problems are raised with advances in **genetic engineering**, a research activity entailing the manipulation of genes.

Heredity and Behavior:

To learn more about the influence of genetic and environmental factors on development, researchers employ: 1) **animal models**, in which the investigator can control both breeding patterns (e.g., **selective breeding experiments** where animals evidencing similarity on particular trait are mated) and environments; 2) **twin studies**, in which the degree of association or concordance on a particular trait is compared for **identical**, or **monozygotic twins**, and **fraternal**, or **dizygotic twins**. Identical twins share all of their genetic material but fraternal twins share, on average, 50 percent of their genetic material. Thus, to the extent that these two kinds of twin pairs show different rates of concordance on particular traits, the difference is believed to be a function of genetic heritability. When monozygotic twins are reared apart, similarities are attributed to genotype and differences are attributed to environment. However, their environments are often quite similar, so that even though they do not grow up together, they may share similar backgrounds; 3) **adoption studies** can also elucidate gene-environment transaction. To the extent that the adoptive child's phenotype is more similar to the biological parents than the adoptive parents the traits are believed to be primarily determined by genetic transmission (i.e., genotype). Similarities between the adoptive child and adoptive parents are attributed to social transmission (i.e., environment); and 4) **consanguinity studies** involve as many relatives as possible in a family in order to discover the degree to which they share a particular trait and whether the closeness of the relationships between individuals affects the degree of similarity.

Using all of these methods, considerable research has been conducted on the heritability of intellectual abilities, personality, and mental illness. For each of these aspects of development, it is clear that genetic factors make a significant contribution to individual differences. At the same time, it is clear that environmental factors also play a major role. Interestingly, for many aspects of behavior, when children are tested over time, heritability ratios increase substantially as the children grow and develop.

KEY TERMS AND CONCEPTS

Answers can be found at the end of this chapter.

1. When a child carries matching alleles for a given trait, she is said to be _____ for that trait.

2. The division of reproductive cells is accomplished through _____.

3. Behaviors are said to be _____ if they are virtually dictated by a prescribed genetic course.

4. _____ twins are identical.

5. Asexual reproduction is called _____.

6. Hemophilia is a sex linked, _____ disorder.

7. In _____, part of a chromosome attaches itself to another chromosome.

8. Somatic cells divide through _____.

9. In males, the 23rd chromosome is _____.

10. The syndrome of retardation and physical anomalies linked to a constricted or broken X-chromosome is called _____ syndrome.

MULTIPLE CHOICE SELF-TEST

Check your answers against those at the end of the chapter.

_____1. The process by which reproductive cells divide is
a. meiosis
b. mitosis
c. canalization
d. pleiotropy

_____2. Sickle-cell anemia
a. affects only females
b. affects only French Canadians
c. is always fatal
d. has a positive evolutionary value in some regions

_____3. Asexual reproduction is called
a. selective breeding
b. meiosis
c. cloning
d. mitosis

_____4. The prenatal test in which cells are sampled from the outer layer of the amniotic sac is called
a. amniocentesis
b. percutaneous umbilical sampling
c. chorionic villus sampling
d. MSAFP screening

_____5. A mathematical estimate of the proportion of trait variance having a genetic origin is the _____ ratio.
a. intelligence quotient
b. heritability
c. consanguinity
d. karyotype

_____6. Women lacking the sex chromosome X have
                 _____ syndrome.
    a.   Turner's
    b.   Down's
    c.   Fragile X
    d.   Klinefelter's

_____7.   In translocation,
    a.   affected individuals lack sex chromosomes
    b.   part of a chromosome attaches itselfht to another
    c.   affected individuals produce abnormal
          hemoglobin
    d.   chromosomal changes are invariably fatal

_____8.   The most common severe genetic disease of
             childhood is
    a.   Down Syndrome
    b.   PKU
    c.   cystic fibrosis
    d.   multiple sclerosis

_____9.   A person whose gene expression has been tered
             to resemble another genotype is a
    a.   phenocopy
    b.   genocopy
    c.   karyotype
    d.   clone

_____10.   A child whose parents are both heterozygous for
             a given trait, S or s, could be
    a.   SS, Ss, or ss
    b.   SS only
    c.   Ss only
    d.   SS or ss only

RECOMMENDATIONS FOR FURTHER READING

Wingerson, L. (1990). Mapping Our Genes: The Genome Project and the Future of Medicine. New York: Plume.

Diamond, M.C. (1988). Enriching Heredity: The Impact of the Environment on the Anatomy of the Brain. New York: The Free Press.

Plomin, R. (1990). Nature and Nurture: An Introduction to Human Behavioral Genetics. Pacific Grove, CA: Brooks/Cole.

Plomin, R., & Daniels, D. (1987). Why are children in the same family so different from one another?, Behavioral and Brain Sciences, 10, 1-60.

Plomin, R., DeFries, J.C., & McClearn, G.E. (1990). Behavior Genetics: A Primer, Second Edition. New York: W. H. Freeman.

ANSWER KEY FOR SELF-TEST ITEMS

Key Terms and Concepts

1.	homozygous	6.	recessive
2.	meiosis	7.	translocation
3.	canalized	8.	mitosis
4.	monozygotic	9.	XY
5.	cloning	10.	Fragile X

Multiple Choice

1.	a	6.	a
2.	d	7.	b
3.	c	8.	c
4.	c	9.	a
5.	b	10.	a

CHAPTER 4

PRENATAL DEVELOPMENT AND BIRTH

STUDY GOALS

After reviewing Chapter 4, you should have a basic understanding of:

1.   Conception and the stages of prenatal development, and what occurs during each. How teratogens, diseases, maternal age, genetic, nutritional, and emotional factors can affect prenatal development.

2.   Social issues related to pregnancy, risks presented to women and young children by poverty, and policies and programs oriented towards the amelioration of such problems.

3.   The 3 stages of childbirth, the risks to the infant inherent in the labor and delivery process, and the range of birthing options available in the U.S., as well as their implications for families.

4.   Developmental and social issues related to prematurity, and the effects of interventions aimed at supporting the preemie and his family.

5.   The interactions among genetic, physiological, environmental, and social factors in determining the outcome of pregnancy and birth, the child's successful integration into the family, and the parents' smooth transition to parenthood.

CHAPTER OVERVIEW

Prenatal Development:

Conception. Approximately once each month, on about the 14th day of a woman's 28-day menstrual cycle, a mature ovum is released from the ovary and arrives in the fallopian tube. If a man's sperm traverses the difficult journey past the cervix to the fallopian tube to reach the egg and penetrates the ovum, their nuclei join together to form a gamete. The sperm that arrive in the fallopian tube undergo a process called **capacitation**, involving the production of enzymes that enable the sperm to dissolve the outer membrane surrounding the egg cell and penetrate its center. Once a single sperm penetrates the egg cell the outer membrane changes such that no penetration by other sperm is possible. The timing of fertilization is precise. The egg cell lives approximately 24 hours in the fallopian tube and the sperm, once deposited, can survive approximately 48 hours.

Upon fertilization, the **zygote** begins the process of cell division and the journey from the fallopian tube to the uterus where it implants itself into the **decidua**, the thickened lining of the uterine wall. Rapid growth ensues and by 8 weeks a recognizable embryonic baby (approximately one inch long) is present in a bag of fluid called the **amniotic sac**. The amniotic sac is comprised of two membranes: the **chorion**, or outer sac, encloses the **amnion**, which contains the amniotic fluid. The nine months in utero are divided into three stages:

1) the **period of the ovum**, which lasts two weeks post-conception during which time the zygote is established in the wall of the uterus;

2) the **period of the embryo**, which lasts until the first occurrence of **ossification**, the formation of solid bone, in the embryo (8 weeks post-conception). This is the period of greatest risk for spontaneous abortion. Differentiation of important organs occurs as the inner mass of the zygote differentiates into three layers (**ectoderm**, **mesoderm**, and **endoderm**). The period of the embryo is also characterized by the development of supporting structures such as the placenta, or afterbirth, the umbilical cord, and the amniotic sac. The placenta is a fleshy disc growing on part of the chorion that permits the passage of substances from the maternal blood stream to that of the fetus. Many substances pass through the **placental barrier**, including important nutrients and hazardous substances such as drugs which may harm the fetus. The **umbilical cord** joins the embryo to the placenta at the abdomen and carries blood through umbilical arteries to the placenta and back through umbilical veins. The **amniotic sac** contains the amniotic fluid

37

which supports the embryo as it moves and protects it against physical shock; and

3) the **period of the fetus**, which lasts from the beginning of the third month until birth. Muscular and central nervous system development occurs at a rapid rate and various body parts become more differentiated. At 26 to 28 weeks post-conception, the fetus enters **the age of viability**, because fetal development is sufficiently advanced so that if birth occurs, the child can survive without major medical intervention.

Sensory Capacities before Birth:

Sensory capacities such as hearing develop before birth. Further, infants' capacity to learn within the womb is demonstrated by their increased activity level in response to their mother's voice in the first 24 hours of life.

Environmental Influences on Prenatal Development:

While the odds are in favor of delivering a normal healthy child, the prenatal period appears to be a **critical period** (a time of heightened sensitivity) for exposure to **teratogens**, environmental agents (e.g., drugs) or other adverse agents (e.g., malnutrition) which can produce abnormalities and malformations in the developing fetus. The first trimester is an especially vulnerable time as the basic structure of the organism is emerging. Different organs are particularly vulnerable at different points in time according to when they begin and end their development (e.g., eyes -- 20-50 days post-conception; heart -- 20-40 days post-conception). Social implications emerge from the study of teratogens, as specific interventions can be employed to avoid the deleterious consequences of exposure. Exposure to a teratogen may not affect all individuals; some individuals have a genetic predisposition to the effect of a particular teratogen or other adverse factors which others do not. Further, other factors, such as maternal age, may interact with a teratogen to influence development. Thus, infants of very young or older mothers may be particularly susceptible. It is not totally clear whether this is truly a function of

38

maternal age or conditions associated with maternal age (e.g., adolescent mothers may not receive adequate health care or nutrition; older women may have been exposed to more environmental agents and may have poorer health status).

The variations in the degree to which the influence of a specific teratogen influences development occurs along a **continuum of reproductive casualty.** Following birth, the **continuum of caretaking casualty** will also influence the extent to which the effects of a teratogen or any other adverse influence will be manifest. Approximately 10 percent of all children are born with some kind of handicap. However, many of these handicaps will disappear entirely due to a strong self-righting mechanism in the human organism toward development. However, a less than adequate environment will contribute to the retention of the handicap. For this reason, researchers are especially concerned about children living in conditions of poverty. The associated harmful conditions include malnutrition, poor sanitation, inadequate shelter, and lack of adequate health care. Further, the parents' reaction to a child's handicapping condition can exacerbate or minimize the extent to which the handicapping condition interferes with the child's development.

Known teratogens include: Radiation (X-rays), chemicals (e.g., household cleaning fluids), industrial pollution, prescription (e.g., iodine and acne medication) and non-prescription drugs (e.g., heroin, cocaine), high consumption of caffeine, smoking (deprives the infant of oxygen), and alcohol (Fetal Alcohol Syndrome). Maternal drug abuse may have different effects depending on the drug or drugs which are ingested: some drugs are addictive and result in withdrawal symptoms in the newborn baby; others are toxic and can cause malformations and/or prematurity; additional indirect risk is from the mother's behavior, which can result in harm to the baby either before or after birth.

Legal Implications:

Across the country, women face criminal charges of child abuse for using drugs or alcohol and thereby placing their unborn babies at risk. In all but one of these cases, charges against the women were dismissed -- primarily because most states do not consider a fetus a child, and child abuse statutes do not cover fetal abuse. Public health groups advocate increasing accessibility to treatment programs and argue that since currently many drug treatment programs exclude pregnant women, punitive legal measures are unlikely to encourage them to seek treatment, and may have the opposite effect.

Diseases of the Mother:

Some infectious diseases contracted by the pregnant mother may cross the placental barrier and affect the developing fetus (e.g., smallpox, measles, chicken pox, mumps, scarlet fever, tuberculosis, malaria, herpes, syphilis and Acquired Immune Deficiency Syndrome - AIDS). In cases such as syphilis, the disease does not affect the fetus under 18 weeks of age. Antibiotics early in pregnancy can prevent injury to the fetus. Other diseases which are not transmissible can also influence fetal development (e.g., diabetes, toxemia).

Genetic Problems:

Rh Factor. Incompatibility between the mother's blood (Rh negative) and that of the infant (Rh positive) is another potentially hazardous problem. The problem involves a buildup of antibodies in the mother's bloodstream against the fetus. First-born babies are typically unaffected, but by the second pregnancy the accumulation of antibodies has a toxic effect on the fetus causing miscarriage or mental retardation. Appropriate treatment can avoid these problems.

Maternal Emotions:

There is increasing evidence that psychological stress can lead to prematurity, low birth weight, and infant behavioral characteristics.

Nutrition:

The pregnant woman's diet and previous nutritional status play significant roles in fetal development. Malnutrition affects all aspects of fetal development, including brain development. It can be especially harmful if malnutrition occurs during a period in which the brain undergoes accelerated growth, or a **growth spurt**. During the prenatal period the brain grows mainly by cell division. Malnourishment during the prenatal period leads to deficits in brain weight at birth. Between six months and two years, brain growth is characterized by the increase in the size of the brain through a process called **myelination**, which involves the development of a fatty protective covering, or sheath -- myelin -- on nerve fibers.

Social Issues: Poverty, Pregnancy, and Child Development:

There are reports of high infant mortality rates in the United States. Some regions in the country have much higher infant mortality rates than the national average, so that these areas often rival Third World countries in infant mortality. More alarming is that infant mortality rates are twice as high for blacks as for whites. Two-thirds of all infant deaths are associated with low birth weight, which in turn is associated with poor nutrition during pregnancy and other prenatal factors such as smoking and lack of health care.

The WIC Program:

The Supplemental Food Program for Women, Infants and Children (WIC) is a government-sponsored preventive health and nutrition program for pregnant women and young children. Mothers participating in WIC and receiving nutritional supplements had a 21 percent decrease in the incidence of low birth weight in infants and a one-third decrease in infant mortality rates as compared to non-WIC mothers. In addition, children receiving nutritional supplements during the prenatal period through the WIC program have higher cognitive functioning and behavioral adaptation 5-7 years later.

The Birth Process:

The birth process occurs in three overlapping stages:

1. increasingly intense uterine contractions begin to cause the cervix to widen until it becomes large enough for the baby to pass through (approximately 12-24 hours);

2.   the baby's head begins to pass through the
cervix and the mother is advised to "push" with her
abdominal muscles until the baby is completely
outside the mother's body (approximately 2 hours);
3.   the placenta and umbilical cord are expelled and
the umbilical cord is cut.

Evaluating the Newborn:

The Apgar scoring system is used at one minute and
five minutes after birth to evaluate heart rate,
respiratory effort, reflex irritability, muscle tone and
body color (score of 0,1,or 2 each).   The higher the
score the more favorable the baby's condition.

Birthing Options:

Practices such as **natural childbirth** (abstaining
from anesthetic medications), the **Lamaze method**
(receiving training in breathing and relaxation
techniques to reduce pain), **rooming in** (hospital rooms in
which mother and infant can remain together) and **birthing
rooms** (homelike rooms where both labor and delivery take
place) are now widely available.   These trends are in
part in response to research in the 1970s on mother-
infant "bonding," which suggested that extended contact
with the mother was necessary in the first hours/days of
life because this is a critical period in the development
of secure attachments.   Recent research has not supported
this notion.

Risks to Infants During Delivery:

While a majority of infants are born through vaginal
deliveries, sometimes a **cesarean section** (surgically
removing the infant from the uterus) is necessary because
the infant is not making adequate progress through the
birth canal or the health status of the mother or infant
is compromised by continuing the labor process.
The two major dangers to the infant during delivery are
1)   pressures on the head, which may cause some blood
vessels in the brain to break, resulting in hemorrhaging,
and 2)   lack of sufficient oxygen once the infant is
separated from the mother.   Both influence the supply of
oxygen to the nerve cells of the brain and may compromise
later development (i.e., cognitive and motor deficits).

42

Prematurity and Low Birth Weight:

Seven percent of all infants in the U.S. are born prematurely (before the end of the 37th week of gestation), but premature infants account for 50% of all infant deaths. Many premature infants develop jaundice or breathing difficulties and some may be developmentally delayed. A majority of premature infants will catch up as they develop. However, in the early months they are more irritable and less easy to soothe than full-term newborns. Parents of premature infants are subjected to many stressors and may need emotional support. Hospital based programs and mutual support groups are available to help parents.

The Positive Effects of Early Intervention Programs:

Early intervention programs for premature and low-birth-weight infants and their parents lead to better social and intellectual functioning. While these programs can be expensive, it may be cheaper to intervene early than to pay for many more years of remedial education.

Social Aspects of Pregnancy and Birth:

Parents have many conflicting feelings about the birth of a new baby. The value placed on the birth of a child and the associated feelings are influenced by the culture and social climate of the time as well as the economy of a particular society. Researchers note that many American parents may have immature expectations of parenthood (being nurtured by the child, having fun). The reality, in terms of demands and responsibilities of caring for an infant, may provoke anger and disappointment. For this reason, many hospitals and schools are offering courses on parenting.

KEY TERMS AND CONCEPTS

Answers can be found at the end of this chapter.

1. The _____ permits the passage of certain substances from the maternal to the fetal bloodstream.

2. Severe oxygen deprivation experienced by the fetus during labor and delivery is called _____.

3. _____ is the fatty coating that protects nerve fibers in the brain.

4. The second stage of prenatal development is called the period of the _____.

5. _____ factor problems result from an incompatibility between maternal and fetal blood.

6. The _____ program provides food supplements to pregnant women and young children.

7. Newborn health status is assessed immediately after birth with the _____ scoring system.

8. In the '60s and '70s it was believed that the first few minutes after birth represented a critical period for mother-infant _____.

9. The teratogenic effects of the drug _____ were often not apparent until the daughters of women who took it reached adulthood.

10. _____ occurs on the 14th day of a woman's menstrual cycle.

MATCHING EXERCISES

Solutions can be found at the end of this chapter.

1.	Dick-Read	a.	food supplements
2.	Lamaze	b.	gentle birth
3.	Leboyer	c.	newborn assessment
4.	WIC	d.	mother-infant bonding
5.	Apgar	e.	Childbirth Without Fear
6.	Klaus & Kennel	f.	breathing exercises, labor coaches

MULTIPLE CHOICE SELF-TEST

Answers can be found at the end of this chapter.

_____1. Differentiation of organs begins during which prenatal stage?
a. embryonic
b. ovum
c. zygote
d. fetal

_____2. A preventable syndrome which causes retardation and may be characterized by facial characteristics such as a low nasal bridge and a narrow upper lip is
a. toxemia
b. FAS
c. phocomelia
d. toxoplasmosis

_____3. At birth the infant
a. is completely deaf
b. can recognize the sound of its mother's voice
c. can hear only voices
d. cannot yet hear voices

_____4. At term, a baby is considered to be low birth
weight if smaller than
a. 4000 grams
b. about 8 pounds
c. about 5 pounds
d. the median weight for full term infants

_____5. The egg cell can survive in the fallopian tube
for about
a. 48 hours
b. 12 hours
c. 24 hours
d. 36 hours

_____6. Central nervous system development is completed
a. during the 1st trimester
b. during the 2nd trimester
c. during the 3rd trimester
d. after birth

_____7. Syphilis causes the greatest damage if the
exposure occurs during
a. the first trimester
b. the first month of pregnancy
c. the first week of pregnancy
d. the last 22 weeks of pregnancy

_____8. The risk of neural tube defects can be sharply
reduced by
a. using multivitamins
b. avoiding smoking during pregnancy
c. avoiding sweets during pregnancy
d. taking exercise classes for pregnant women

_____9. In prevention of infant mortality, the U.S.
ranks _____ in the world.
a. 3rd
b. 19th
c. 1st
d. 53rd

_____10. Uterine contractions cause widening of the
cervix during the
a. 1st
b. 2nd
c. 3rd
d. 1st and 3rd

SUGGESTIONS FOR FURTHER READING

Blatt, R. J. R. (1988). Prenatal Tests: What They Are, Their Benefits and Risks, and How to Decide Whether to Have Them or Not. New York: Vintage Books.

Dorris, M. (1989). The Broken Cord [fetal alcohol syndrome]. New York: Harper & Row.

Kopp, C. (1983). Risk factors in development. In M. M. Haith & J. Campos (Eds.), Handbook of Child Psychology (4th ed.). Infancy and Developmental Psychobiology (pp. 1081-1188). New York: John Wiley and Sons.

Molfese, V. J. (1989). Perinatal Risk and Infant Development. New York: Guilford Press.

Nilsson, L. (1965). A Child Is Born. New York: Delta.

ANSWER KEY FOR SELF-TEST ITEMS

Key Terms and Concepts

1.	placenta	6.	WIC
2.	anoxia	7.	Apgar
3.	myelin	8.	bonding
4.	embryo	9.	DES
5.	Rh	10.	ovulation

Matching

1-e; 2-f; 3-b; 4-a; 5-c; 6-d

Multiple Choice

1.	a	6.	d
2.	b	7.	d
3.	b	8.	a
4.	c	9.	b
5.	c	10.	a

CHAPTER 5

PHYSICAL DEVELOPMENT DURING INFANCY

STUDY GOALS

The student should be able to do the following after studying Chapter 5.

1. Describe the appearance, behavior, and states of the newborn; grasp the relationship among state, behavior, and mother-infant interaction.

2. Explain the sensory and perceptual capabilities of the normal newborn, and the effect that impairments in these capacities can have on development.

3. Explain the major ways in which atypical forms of development occur, and how early intervention programs can help to ameliorate the negative consequences of such atypical development.

4. Describe the respective roles of biology and environment in the unfolding of infant development.

5. Explore the roles of government and social policy in issues pertaining to infant development.

CHAPTER OVERVIEW

THE NEWBORN BABY

Characteristics of the Newborn Baby:

Although largely dependent on adult care, the newborn has a range of capacities for responding to environmental stimuli.

Appearance:

Immediately after birth the newborn has several qualities that make him or her appear quite fragile and sometimes odd. These include: a short neck, an oily substance covering the body called **vernix caseosa, lanugo** (some babies are covered with fine-textured hair all over their bodies), a bulging abdomen, and broad, flat face. Other features make babies of all species quite attractive (e.g., large head relative to body, large eyes, small nose) and may trigger affectionate feelings in adults which promote survival.

Individuality:

There is marked variability between newborns in appearance and behavior which is a function of prenatal and delivery experiences as well as genetic endowment. Variability in genetic endowment can be seen by looking at groups of infants who are more similar genetically. Thus, some of the variability in infant behavior can be explained as a function of infant sex (e.g., boys are more active than girls), and race (e.g., Chinese-American infants are more easily calmed than infants of European descent). **Temperament**, a broad term referring to the individual's pattern of response to the environment, also shows marked variability. Both genetic and environmental contributions to temperament have been documented. Thomas and Chess argued that while some infant temperaments are in general "easy" or "difficult," in order for any child to develop normally and adjust to their environment, there has to be a **goodness of fit**, or a match between children's temperament and the demands that are placed on the children.

Infant Reflexes:

Reflexes are specific, involuntary responses to stimuli. The baby is born with many reflexes which will disappear after the first several months of life. **Adaptive reflexes**, such as coughing, sucking, blinking, **rooting** (especially when hungry, babies will turn in the direction of a cheek which is touched) and crying, are present from birth and ensure a baby's survival. Other reflexes do not appear to have immediate survival value (e.g., the **Moro reflex**, or **startle reflex**). Some reflexes, such as grasping and walking, are present at birth but disappear and come under the volitional control of the infant. Our knowledge of infant reflexes is the basis for the neurological assessment of newborns. The absence of any of the reflexes may indicate a serious developmental disturbance.

Infant States:

Infant **state** refers to the extent to which the baby is asleep or aroused. Newborns sleep most of the day (16-20 hours), but their sleep/wake cycles are not well regulated. Half of the newborn sleeping hours are spent in rapid eye movement (REM) sleep (characterized by fluctuations, blood pressure, and brain waves and associated with dreaming in older children and adults). **Autostimulation theory** suggests that during REM sleep there is spontaneous neurological firing in the brain which stimulates higher brain centers and may stimulate the development of the central nervous system. By six months of age, most infants will sleep through the night. To maximally benefit from information in the environment, infants must be in an alert, quiet state. Infants will change from one state to another to regulate the amount of stimulation they receive (e.g., avert gaze, cry, sleep). The **Brazelton Neonatal Behavioral Assessment Scale** assesses the behavior of infants in relation to the states they are in and examines infants' capacity for interaction.

Influencing Infant State/Soothing:

The state parents most want to change is infant crying. The quieter and calmer the baby, the more able he or she is to become acquainted with the environment. Babies cry for many reasons (e.g., hunger, pain, overstimulation, restlessness). While crying serves a communication value, parents often have difficulty distinguishing different kinds of crying. There are many means to soothe a crying infant. These include: feeding, swaddling (wrapping the child in a blanket), walking or rocking the baby, letting the baby rest and introducing a rhythmic sound.

SENSORY AND PERCEPTUAL CAPABILITIES OF THE INFANT

Sensation refers to the ability to detect a certain stimulus in the environment. **Perception** refers to the ability to process or interpret these sensations. Since the 1960s, infancy research has documented that babies are born equipped with acute senses, are capable of making immediate responses to the environment and have limited perceptual skills.

To study these capacities, researchers have relied on the assessment of psychophysiology (e.g., changes in heart rate, respiration, and muscle contraction), monitoring gaze to determine visual preferences, and habituation and dishabituation paradigms. **Habituation** is a type of learning indicating that a particular stimulus has become familiar, or learned, and thus no longer elicits interest or attention. **Dishabituation** occurs when the baby notices that a new object is slightly different from a previous familiar object; he or she may evidence interest and attend to the new object.

Hearing:

At birth, the newborn's auditory canals are filled with amniotic fluid; thus for the first day or two hearing may be muffled. Newborn infants can localize sounds and are especially sensitive to high pitched sounds. Newborns are particularly responsive to speech sounds. By 1-2 months of age infants can distinguish speech sounds such as "pa" and "ba" and can distinguish speech sounds which do not occur in their native tongue and which in adulthood they will lose the capacity to distinguish between. Further, they appear to synchronize their movements to the acoustic structure of speech.

Seeing:

At birth, the eyes of the human newborn are physiologically and anatomically ready to respond to many aspects of the visual field and they can distinguish between some colors. However, they have poor **visual acuity**, which is the ability to detect the separate parts of an object and they are unable to focus well at a distance. These skills improve such that at one year of age infants see as clearly as adults do. Color vision is similar to an adult's by four months of age.

Strategies for Looking:

Unlike adults, who look at an entire form, newborns attend only to the edges of a form. By two months of age, newborns attend to the center or internal area of the visual target as well as on its edges. Marshall Haith has found that the baby has visual scanning rules.

Pattern Perception:

With age, infants also improve in their ability to perceive different patterns and shapes. Infants show a clear preference for the face and for patterned forms over other visual forms.

Depth Perception:

Young babies also have some idea of depth. Depth perception may be an innate mechanism, as it protects the young of any species from falling.

Touch, Smell, and Taste:

The experience of being touched has a direct effect on growth and development. Premature infants who are massaged, for example, gain more weight than nonmassaged premature infants even though the caloric intake of the two groups is the same. Newborn smell is also well developed. Newborns can discriminate between a variety of smells and remember smells they have been exposed to. In terms of taste, infants' sucking responses differ depending on whether they are given sweet or salty solutions.

Interconnectedness Among the Senses:

Cross-modal transfer of information refers to the process whereby knowledge gained from one sense is used to inform other senses (e.g., we look toward the location of a sound). Piaget argued that this process is learned through gradual associations. Current research suggests that coordination of the senses may be present from birth.

PHYSICAL GROWTH AND MOTOR DEVELOPMENT

Physical Growth:

Immediately after birth the infant loses some weight; but after the first few days they begin to gain weight and grow at a rapid pace. By the time infants are two years of age they have quadrupled their birth weight and doubled their birth height. **Ossification** (hardening of the bones) continues as does skeletal growth. Three principles govern physical growth: 1) **cephalocaudal sequence**, or that growth occurs from head to toe; 2) **proximodistal direction**, or that development occurs from the center to the extremities; and 3) there is an ordered sequence in the acquisition of motor skills proceeding from the simple to the complex.

The Brain:

For the first six months of life the brain is growing at a very rapid pace, with brain cells increasing in number. After this period, the brain continues to grow, but the changes are more complex than an increase in cell number. There are two kinds of cells in the brain: **Neurons**, or nerve cells, which receive and send impulses or signals and **neuroglia**, also called **glial cells**, which feed and support the nerve cells. In neurons, the cytoplasm is drawn out into a large number of fine, wirelike workings called **dendrites** and **axons**. Dendrites and axons have many branches connecting with other branches that emerge from other cells. Dendrites receive impulses and axons send them. The brain can be divided into three layers: the **forebrain** (**upper cortex**), and **midbrain and hindbrain** (**subcortex**), which make up the brainstem. The brainstem is connected to the rest of the body through the spinal cord. This entire system is the central nervous system. The subcortex develops prior to the upper cortex.

Discussion of Social Issues: Babies Born with AIDS:

AIDS, or Acquired Immune Deficiency Syndrome, is caused by the Human Immunodeficiency Virus (HIV). Pediatric AIDS differs from adult AIDS since most infected children experience central nervous system complications, whereas such problems affect only a small number of infected adults. Due to their immune incompetence, they cannot ward off childhood diseases. Infants infected with AIDS also experience retarded and abnormal growth and have abnormal facial features (e.g., small head, big eyes, a flat nose, and a prominent forehead).

Recently, a U.S. House Select Committee on Children, Youth, and Families (1989) called for increased spending for education, research, testing, and treatment to fight pediatric AIDS.

53

Motor Development:

Motor is the term used to denote muscular movement, and motor development is the process through which the child acquires movement patterns and skills. Babies develop increasing control over a variety of differentiated movements. These new abilities are then integrated into more complex behavior patterns (**hierarchic integration**). Motor development follows a cephalocaudal and proximodistal pattern. While most babies follow the sequence of motor development, the age at which a particular skill will emerge in a given child is subject to considerable variability. For example, a child may begin to walk at 8 months or 15 months. Walking is a major milestone in the baby's development, but often too much importance is attached to this achievement. Early walking is not associated with superior intelligence.

Learning From Other Cultures:

The role of maturation and environment is highlighted in cross-cultural research. In these studies, all children tend to evidence the same sequence and schedule of motor development. This led researchers to believe that maturation played a significant role in motor development. However, other studies, (e.g., of infants in orphanages) reveal that some environmental stimulation is necessary.

ATYPICAL DEVELOPMENT

The Birth of Severely Disabled Infants:

Medical technology has advanced to a point when many disabled infants who would otherwise die can now be saved. Often they live to face a life of physical suffering or severe disability. Complex ethical and legal dilemmas therefore exist regarding who decides whether or not to determine the babies' fate (i.e., parents, physicians, or the legal system).

Identifying the Disabled Infant:

In 1986 Congress enacted a law (PL-99-457, Part H), Services for Infants and Toddlers with Handicapping

Conditions, to ensure identification of infants as early in life as possible. Several new screening instruments have been developed to facilitate this goal.

Infants at Risk:

Risks compromising the newborn's development are diverse and include risks of biological origin, environmental origin, and others which arise from a combination of the two. Not all infants identified as at risk are equally vulnerable. Some will develop normally, while others, especially those whose families experience stressful life events and circumstances, may be unable to overcome their disability.

Developmentally Disabled Infants:

Screening tests are also used to identify infants suffering from a developmental disability. This is a chronic disorder which can be manifest in mental or physical impairment.

Visual Impairments:

Infants who are born blind or with severe visual impairments are slow to acquire mobility skills and while they acquire cognitive, language, and social skills in much the same sequence as sighted infants, they do evidence developmental delays. These delays are understood primarily in terms of "experiential poverty." Providing auditory and other sensory cues to encourage blind infants to move and talk appears to promote development.

Hearing Impairments:

Often, diagnosis of a hearing impairment in an infant is not made until the second year of life because hearing-impaired infants babble. Research with this population has been limited, but available evidence suggests that hearing-impaired infants do not progress in auditory discrimination, and show significant problems in language acquisition. Hearing aids and sign language can minimize the negative impact of the disability on the child's development.

Cerebral Palsy:

Cerebral palsy, characterized by muscle weakness, paralysis, incoordination, or aberration of motor dysfunction, results from brain damage suffered during the pre- or perinatal period. A majority of children with cerebral palsy have additional handicapping conditions. For example, 70-80 percent have speech and language problems and many suffer from severe visual impairment, learning disabilities, and seizures. Some are mentally retarded.

Services for At-Risk and Disabled Infants:

1. Disabled infants are a heterogeneous group who differ in level of disability as well as in temperament and ability to compensate for the disability.
2. Disabled infants are competent and active learners who should be given the opportunity to feel mastery in their environments.

Early Intervention:

There is a wide range of types of early intervention programs including home-based teaching, center-based (hospital, school, mental health clinic), and family support services. Successful early intervention not only focuses on the infant but also includes the parents. In addition to teaching the parents specific parenting skills to promote development and help their disabled infant compensate for the disability, parents of disabled infants need emotional support to cope with the ramifications of living with a disabled child.

KEY TERMS AND CONCEPTS

Fill in the blank with the word or phrase that best completes the sentence. Check your answers at the end of this chapter.

1. The white, oily coating that protects a baby's skin <u>in utero</u> is called _____.

2. An individual infant's way of responding to the environment is called _____.

3. _____ are specific, involuntary responses to stimuli.

4. When a newborn's cheek is touched gently, she will turn her head in the direction of the touched cheek. This is called the _____ reflex.

5. The degree to which an infant is sleepy or aroused at any given time is his _____.

6. _____ is defined as the cessation or marked diminution of a response to a stimulus after a number of presentations of that stimulus.

7. Growth which follows a head to toe pattern is said to follow a _____ sequence.

8. The function of _____ is to receive impulses in the nervous system.

9. The function of _____ is to send them.

10. The forebrain is known as the _____.

MATCHING EXERCISE

Match the name to the idea, accomplishment, or area of research.

1. Chess & Thomas
2. Brazelton
3. DeVries & Sameroff
4. Condon & Sander
5. Fantz
6. Selma Fraiberg

a. infant temperament
b. cross-cultural studies of attachment
c. smiling in blind infants
d. infant visual perception
e. infant states and behavior
f. infant responses to speech

MULTIPLE CHOICE SELF-TEST

_____1. The fine hair which sometimes covers the skin of newborns is
a. vernix caseosa
b. lanugo
c. ossification
d. "baby acne"

_____2. Infants sometimes arch their backs suddenly and fling their arms wide. This is the _____ reflex.
a. Moro
b. Babinski
c. startle
d. rooting

_____3. The average newborn sleeps for
a. the whole night, and is awake all day
b. the day, and is awake all night
c. about 8 hours out of 24
d. about 16-20 hours out of 24

_____ 4. An infant who gradually loses interest after repeated presentations of the same stimulus is demonstrating
   a. habituation
   b. the Moro reflex
   c. dishabituation
   d. cephalocaudal sequence

_____ 5. A newborn scanning a human face focuses primarily on
   a. the mouth
   b. the eyes
   c. the color of the skin
   d. any movement, such as a speaking mouth

_____ 6. Depth perception in infants is studied using
   a. a black and white image of a face
   b. a still face photo of the infant's mother
   c. the visual cliff apparatus
   d. a Fantz box

_____ 7. The fine, wirelike impulse transmitters of nerve cells are called
   a. axons
   b. dendrites
   c. neuroglia
   d. glial cells

_____ 8. La Leche League provides
   a. pregnant women with food supplements
   b. birth control and abortion counseling
   c. information and support for women who breastfeed
   d. prepared childbirth classes

_____ 9. The Brazelton Neonatal Behavioral Assessment Scale measures
   a. the infant's health status at 1 and 5 minutes after birth
   b. infant temperament
   c. infant reflexes
   d. state-related behaviors and the infant's capacity for interaction

_____10. The most common cause of infant death between
          one week and one year of age in the U.S. is
a. cerebral palsy
b. SIDS
c. malnutrition
d. influenza

RECOMMENDATIONS FOR FURTHER READING

Brazelton, T. B. (1985). Infants and Mothers. New York:
Delta.

Brazelton, T. B. (1990). Saving the bathwater [neonatal
development and measurement]. Child Development, 61,
1661-1671.

Bronson, G. W. (1991). Infant differences in rate of
visual encoding. Child Development, 62, 44-45.

Landry, S. H., Chapieski, M., Richardson, M. A., Palmer,
J., et al. (1990). The social competence of children born
prematurely: Effects of medical complications and parent
behaviors. Child Development, 61, 1605-1616.

Meisels, S., & Shonkoff, J. (Eds.) (1990). Handbook of
Early Childhood Intervention. New York: Cambridge
University Press.

Olds, D. L., & Kitzman, H. (1990). Can home intervention
improve the health of women and children at environmental
risk? Pediatrics, 86, 108-116.

ANSWER KEY FOR SELF-TEST ITEMS

Key Terms and Concepts

1. vernix caseosa
2. temperament
3. reflexes
4. rooting
5. state

6. habituation
7. cephalocaudal
8. dendrites
9. axons
10. upper cortex

Matching

1-a; 2-e; 3-b; 4-f; 5-d; 6-c

Multiple Choice

1. b   6. c
2. c   7. a
3. d   8. c
4. a   9. d
5. b   10. b

CHAPTER 6

COGNITIVE AND LANGUAGE DEVELOPMENT IN INFANCY

STUDY GOALS

In reading and reviewing Chapter 6, you should develop an understanding of:

1. The tenets and methods of the major approaches to the study of cognition in infancy: behaviorism (including classical and operant conditioning), Piaget's work and theories, the theories of Noam Chomsky, and information processing.

2. The basics of language development, including milestones and early sounds, and the major approaches to the origins and development of language.

3. The role parents play in the cognitive development of infants, and the implications for pushing early formal learning in infancy.

4. The types of substitute care available for infants, and how high-quality child care for infants is defined; what the research tells us about the effect of substitute child care during infancy.

CHAPTER OVERVIEW

COGNITIVE DEVELOPMENT

Learning in Early Life:

   Learning is defined as a relatively permanent change in behavior occurring as a result of experience. Learning can occur in several ways, through classical conditioning, operant conditioning, observation, and imitation.

Classical Conditioning:

   Classical conditioning is a basic mechanism through which the individual learns about associations between events. Pavlov, a Russian physiologist, first reported about this phenomenon in his experiments with dogs. He noted that a **conditioned stimulus** (bell), or neutral stimulus which does not evoke a given response independently, when paired with an **unconditioned stimulus** (sight of food), which evokes an **unconditioned response** or reflex response (salivation), would elicit a **conditioned response** (salivation). Classical conditioning occurs in newborns as young as 2 hours and there are indications that it may occur in utero. However, there is some controversy about these findings because many investigators have failed to replicate them. Findings regarding appear more stable for positive reinforcers, or pleasurable stimuli. Researchers have not been able to demonstrate **aversive conditioning** in young infants.

Operant Conditioning:

In **operant**, or **instrumental conditioning**, a change in the frequency or intensity of behavior occurs as a result of the consequences of behavior, that is, through **reinforcement**. Through this form of learning, infants learn the contingency between their behavior and its consequences. Learning and maturation are interdependent processes. As the infant gets older, he or she has increased learning capabilities, a concept that is termed **learning readiness**.

Memory:

Demonstrating conditioning in young infants indicates not only that infants can learn, but also that they remember, since learning is dependent on memory. Researchers make a distinction between **recognition memory**, identifying something previously known, and **recall memory**, where a given stimulus is not present. Several formal experiments support the notion that recall memory appears only in the latter half of the first year.

Forming categories:

Categorization refers to the ability to mentally organize information into related groupings. Grouping objects greatly reduces the information load on the cognitive system and enhances our ability to respond quickly. Early categorization skills appear to emerge in the latter half of the first year of life. By the end of the first year of life, infants can generate simple categories by choosing objects based on specific properties (e.g., color, shape), but their ability to categorize is perception bound. That is, they categorize on the basis of perceptual rather than functional categories.

APPROACHES TO STUDYING COGNITIVE DEVELOPMENT

Cognition is defined as the act of knowing. It includes learning, thinking, imagining, creating, problem solving, and many other skills associated with intellectual behavior. Developmental psychologists have many ways of studying cognitive behavior. The **psychometric approach**, which began with the development of standardized intelligence testing, is but one of many means of studying changes in cognitive abilities.

Information Processing:

All information processing theories share the assumption that the human mind is a system for storing and retrieving information. In addition, they share the belief that human beings have limited information processing abilities, and that through cognitive growth they gradually reduce these limitations. Limitations may be a function of our ability to attend, capacity for memory, or our facility of output. In studying attention, researchers have focused on two primary measures: **decrement of attention** (i.e., habituation to an unchanged environment) and **recovery of attention**, which infants exhibit when they notice a novel aspect of the environment. Attention in infancy has proven a better predictor of later intellectual functioning than cognitive skills such as memory and problem solving.

The Piagetian Approach:

Piaget is noted for his exploration of cognitive growth as a continuous process beginning at birth and continuing over four major stages: the sensorimotor, preoperational, concrete operational and formal operational periods. The order of progression is invariant, as a new stage builds upon the previous stages. Each stage is associated with a specific age period: infancy, the preschool years, the school-age

64

years and adolescence. In addition, each stage is associated with different **cognitive structures**. Piaget views the individual as an active organism engaged in a dynamic process of acquiring information. **Schemata** (more than one **schema**) are the strategies by which an infant interacts with the environment (e.g., sucking, reaching). With development, these schemata are integrated into increasingly complex actions and are eventually based on mental representations rather than on reflex or motor activity. **Organization** and **adaptation** govern interaction with the environment which in turn leads to the modification of schemata. Adaptation occurs through two complementary processes: **assimilation** and **accommodation**. One goal of adaptation is to achieve equilibrium.

Sensorimotor Period:

This is the first stage in cognitive development and under typical circumstances lasts approximately two years. Interactions with the environment are governed by overt sensory and motor abilities. Gradually, motor representations become mental or symbolic representations as the infant develops the capacity for **object permanence**. The capacity for representational thought allows for much more advanced problem solving. Piaget divided the sensorimotor period into 6 stages.

LANGUAGE DEVELOPMENT

The capacity for mental representation heralds advances in language development.

Theories of Language Acquisition:

Language has three interrelated dimensions: 1) **semantics**, which refers to the meaning of words and sentences; 2) **syntax**, which refers to the rules of sentence formation; and 3) **pragmatics**, how we use language to communicate. For most children, language acquisition progresses from a few words at age two to an adult grammar and vast vocabulary by age five. Most researchers now believe that while the human organism is equipped to learn language (nature), experience with language (nurture) is necessary for language development.

The Learning Theory Approach:

The behaviorist **B.F. Skinner** put forth an extreme position on language learning. Skinner claimed that youngsters learned language through a process of systematic reinforcement by adults. More recent observers have generally dismissed this extreme position even though infants do babble more when their parents respond enthusiastically and parents do play a role in responding to children's language errors by expanding, recasting, or correctly repeating the child's utterance. Learning theory fails to account for why children's emerging language unfolds in a particular sequence and is characterized by systematic errors (e.g., "no sleepy," "mouses"). Learning theory also fails to explain the dramatic changes in learning rates or the apparent ease of language acquisition in the first five years of development (e.g., the rapid acceleration during the preschool years).

Biological Orientation:

Noam Chomsky believes that there is a biological explanation for language learning because of the evidence that across many cultures and languages children acquire language skills (e.g., first word, putting two words together, making sentences) at about the same age. He proposed that the central nervous system contains a mental structure (or module), the **language acquisition device (LAD)**, which enables infants to isolate speech sounds from birth and triggers various speech milestones (e.g., the onset of babbling). Chomsky proposed that there were two levels of structure in language: **surface structure**, which refers to the ordering of words; and **deep structure**, which refers to the meaning or basic relationships between words. The rules connecting surface and deep structure are known as transformational grammar.

Eric Lennenberg, another theorist who adhered to a biological explanation, proposed that language is an inherited species-specific characteristic. That is, humans have evolved with highly specialized mechanisms that predispose them toward learning language and also shape language development. Although apes can learn some language, they cannot learn to speak because they lack the anatomical structures necessary to produce speech sounds. Lennenberg pointed out that infants go through language milestones that are related to brain development.

To follow the progression of milestones from birth it is important to distinguish between **expressive** (productive) and **receptive** language.

Early Sounds:

The first sounds produced in infancy are not random noises. Regardless of the language spoken in the home, the sounds infants make during their first year follow a highly ordered sequence: crying, cooing - 1 month, and then babbling - 6 months. Initially babbling involves simple consonant-vowel syllables repeated in succession (da, da, da, da, ma, ma, ma). Eventually, variegated babbling, which involves variations in the consonants, appears (ba di ba da). Hearing impairment in infancy is often undetected because hearing-impaired infants babble in the same manner as hearing infants. It is critical to identify hearing-impaired infants because they require linguistic input (e.g., exposure to sign language) for their language development to progress appropriately.

Communicating by Sound and Gesture:

After babbling, the infant progresses to a variety of short speech sounds, most often accompanied by gestures (e.g., pointing, reaching), to express a variety of emotions and needs. Most but not all infants go through a spurt in vocabulary acquisition sometime in the second year of life. Infants' early vocabulary includes things they can act on, words for objects and people important in their lives (e.g., Daddy, Mommy, bottle), and specific categories rather than higher order generalities (e.g., flower vs. plant and doggie vs. animal).

The Meaning of Words:

An infant may say and use a word appropriately but not have exactly the same meaning for the word as older children and adults. For example, a father may be excited to be called "dada" but chagrined when his infant refers to all men with this label. Overextensions such as this are very common.

Holophrastic Speech:

Holophrastic speech refers to the impression that first words appear to be attempts to express complex ideas. Thus, "go" may mean: "Let's go outside now." Non-verbal gestures often accompany these one-word utterances to clarify the infant's intention.

Combining Words:

At 18-20 months of age, infants begin to combine words. They typically use nouns, verbs, and adjectives, but omit articles and prepositions (e.g., "truck go" instead of "The truck is going"). For this reason, two-year-old speech is sometimes referred to as **telegraphic speech**. Topics are typically limited to concrete aspects of the environment.

NEW WAYS INFANTS ARE GROWING UP TODAY

Now that the media has disseminated some of the newer research findings on infants' cognitive capacities -- especially learning abilities -- some individuals and parents are advocating teaching toddlers academic skills (e.g., reading and arithmetic). There is no evidence that kits which include flashcards intended to teach infants to read succeed. In fact, reading to children is probably the best vehicle for teaching the pre-reading skills that lay the foundation for later reading. These activities can also take away precious time for playful interaction with infants and allowing them to manipulate objects in their environment. It is through interaction and manipulation that infants develop a sense of personal connection and effectiveness.

Early Experience and Later Life:

Infants growing up in conditions of perceptual and socially impoverished environments (e.g., orphanages in the past) are likely to suffer significant difficulties in social, emotional and intellectual development.

The Role of Parents in Cognitive Development:

Parents who direct their infant's attention, hold, touch, smile at, and talk to their infants a great deal are more likely to have infants who are more advanced cognitively than other infants who do not receive this attention.

DISCUSSION OF SOCIAL ISSUES: INFANTS IN OUT-OF-HOME GROUP CARE

With the increase in single-parent families and the need or choice of both parents to work outside the home full-time -- more parents than ever before are in the work force and obliged to find suitable child care for their babies. Child care for infants is of special concern because: 1) there is a shortage of quality child care facilities in our country; and 2) an infant is more dependent on the caregiver, and thus, more vulnerable to adversity than an older child.

What the Research Tells Us About Infants in Child Care:

There is a great deal of debate and controversy about whether the infant should be raised by her own parents or by other caretakers. Unfortunately, the research on this issue is still inconclusive. Recently, however, panel members of the National Research Council stated that there is no reason for parents to be urged toward or away from enrolling their children in child care; attention should be addressed toward the quality of care and its impact on child development.

What Is Quality Care?

Do infants receive adequate care when the following conditions are met?
1) infants have adequate opportunities to play with and interact with adults;
2) infants receive adequate nutrition and health care;
3) there is a good staff:infant ratio to insure that each infant receives individualized attention;
4) caregivers are educated about and sensitive to the developmental needs of the infants; and
5) there is consistency in caregivers (i.e., low staff turnover).

Realities of Child Care in the United States:

State regulations governing child care vary from state to state. These regulations typically address

69

issues such as staff:child ratios, group size, and other quality indicators designed to measure safety and health (e.g., building codes). In all states, these regulations concern minimal standards rather than ensuring quality. Another concern is that a majority of family day care homes are unlicensed and therefore have not been evaluated by even the minimal criteria set forth by states.

KEY TERMS AND CONCEPTS

Check your answers against those at the end of the chapter.

1. An infant who ways "want milk" to mean "I want some milk" is using _____ speech.

2. An infant who says "me" to mean "I want to do that by myself" is using _____ speech.

3. In classical conditioning, the stimulus which, neutral prior to the experiment, comes to produce the desired response is the _____ stimulus.

4. In _____ conditioning, changes in behavior occur as a result of the consequences of behavior.

5. _____ are the strategies by which the infant interacts with the environment.

6. A child who comes to understand that an unfamiliar object actually belongs in a familiar category is engaging in _____.

7. The Piagetian stage represented by infancy is the _____ period.

8. Chomsky's model of the child's innate capacity to structure and process language revolved around the concept of the _____.

9. _____ is the ability to mentally organize information into related groupings.

10. The infant's awareness that objects exist independently of our perceptions of them is called _____.

_____1.   When Pavlov's dogs were conditioned to salivate
            in response to the ringing of a bell, the bell was
       a.   a reward
       b.   the CS
       c.   the UCS
       d.   the conditioned response

_____2.   The _____ dimension of language refers to the
            meaning of words.
       a.   holophrastic
       b.   pragmatic
       c.   semantic
       d.   syntactical

_____3.   Most infants whose mothers are employed outside
            the home are cared for
       a.   in corporate-subsidized infant centers
       b.   by illegal immigrants
       c.   in family day care homes
       d.   at home by their fathers

_____4.   Object permanence is typically acquired around
            age
       a.   12 months
       b.   18 months
       c.   36 months
       d.   4 months

_____5.   A crying infant quiets when he sees his mother
            preparing to feed him. This is an example of
       a.   operant conditioning
       b.   assimilation
       c.   aversive conditioning
       d.   classical conditioning

_____6.   A rat learns to obtain food by pressing a
            lever. This is an example of
       a.   classical conditioning
       b.   operant conditioning
       c.   aversive conditioning
       d.   recall memory

_____ 7.   The Piagetian stage corresponding to infancy is
     a.   preoperational
     b.   concrete operational
     c.   sensorimotor
     d.   formal operational

_____ 8.   The infant who says "Daddy have" to mean "Daddy
           has the ball now" is using _____.
     a.   telegraphic speech
     b.   babbling
     c.   deep structure
     d.   holophrastic speech

_____ 9.   Recommended staff:child ratio for infant day
           care is
     a.   1:3
     b.   1:4
     c.   2:6
     d.   1:8

_____ 10. For Piaget, each period of cognitive
           development involves different
     a.   classifications
     b.   structures
     c.   genders
     d.   accommodation

SUGGESTIONS FOR FURTHER READING

Belsky, J. (1986). Infant day care: A cause for concern? Zero to Three, February, 22-24.

Gamble, T. J., & Zigler, E. (1986). Effects of infant day care: Another look at the evidence. American Journal of Orthopsychiatry, 56, 26-42.

McCartney, K. (Ed.) (1990). Child care and maternal employment: A social ecology approach. New Directions for Child Development, No. 49. San Francisco: Jossey-Bass.

Phillips, D., McCartney, K., Scarr, S., & Howes, C. (1987). Selective review of infant day care: A cause for concern. Zero to Three, 6, 18-24.

Poulson, C. L., Kymissis, E., Reeve, K. F., Andreatos, M., et al. (1991). Generalized vocal imitation in infants. Journal of Experimental Child Psychology, 51, 267-279.

Rossetti, L. M. (1990). Infant-Toddler Assessment: An Interdisciplinary Approach. Boston: College-Hill Press/Little, Brown and Company.

Young, K. T., & Zigler, E. (1986). Infant and toddler day care: Regulations and policy implications. American Journal of Orthopsychiatry, 56, 43-55.

Zigler, E., & Lang, M. (1991). Child Care Choices. New York: The Free Press.

ANSWER KEY FOR SELF-TEST ITEMS

Key Terms and Concepts

1. telegraphic
2. holophrastic
3. conditioned
4. operant
5. schemata

6. accommodation
7. sensorimotor
8. language acquisition device
9. categorization
10. object permanence

Multiple Choice

1. b
2. c
3. c
4. a
5. d

6. b
7. c
8. a
9. a
10. b

CHAPTER 7

SOCIAL AND EMOTIONAL DEVELOPMENT IN INFANCY

STUDY GOALS

While studying Chapter 7, you should strive for an understanding of:

1. What variables contribute to--or impede--sound social and emotional development in infancy. What roles the mother and father play in this developmental course, and how these roles differ.

2. Milestones marking the course of the infant's social/emotional development, including the emergence of smiling, fear, and other aspects of emotional communication.

3. The meaning and development of attachment, and variations in its expression among individual infants and in different cultures. The variables that affect the expression of attachment, and which ones are associated with its optimal development.

4. The effect of social deprivation during infancy, and the possibility of reversing these negative effects.

5. Social policy issues related to social/emotional development during infancy. The role played by the U.S. government in implementing policies conducive to optimal infant/family development.

CHAPTER OVERVIEW

EARLY SOCIAL DEVELOPMENT: BECOMING ACQUAINTED

Infants enter the world with many capacities which prepare them to interact with and influence their social environment. Through social interaction they will develop the capacity to establish emotional connections with others in the world. Emotional development is emphasized in infancy because emotional health will influence many other domains of development.

From birth, infants and parents are partners in social interaction. Indeed, the contribution of infant and parent to the social interaction has been described as a carefully choreographed dance. Each partner synchronizes his or her steps, takes turns, modifies their own behavior and influences the partner's subsequent behaviors. Early on, parents are structuring and leading the interaction, but over time, the infant exerts increasing influence on the nature of the social exchange.

Research on Mother-Infant Interactions:

Mutual modification of behavior within the interaction, which is also called **synchrony** or **reciprocity**, is especially evident in playful interactions. This synchrony depends on the infant's ability to signal her needs, the capacity to respond to the mother's behavior and the mother's ability to read the infant's signals and respond appropriately.

Tuning In to One Another:

Coordinated bouts of synchronous behavior don't occur all of the time and when they do they last for a few minutes. These exciting face-to-face interactions are interspersed with periods of quiet, rest and the daily routines of care (e.g., feeding, diapering).

Barriers to Positive Social Interactions:

Difficulties in early interaction and social development may occur when the mother has difficulty taking care of the baby. The difficulty may be due to the baby's unusual needs (e.g., unresponsive, medically frail, hypersensitive) or because the mother is preoccupied with her own life stresses, emotions and/or responsibilities. Intrusive mothers do not ease off when their infants avert their gaze (a signal that they are overstimulated in the interaction). Instead, they "chase" after the infant's attention by changing the intensity or increasing the frequency of vocalizations and affective expressions and/or the present objects. By these intrusive behaviors the mother denies the infant the opportunity to learn that he can communicate his needs and desires to regulate the world.

Trust vs. Mistrust:

Erik Erikson suggested that a basic sense of trust is a vital aspect of personality development and lays the groundwork for the child's later relationships. This basic sense of trust emerges from the infant's experience with their primary caregiver. In a sensitive, loving, positive environment, the infant will develop an expectancy for trust. In contrast, if the baby's experience is characterized by anger and coldness, it will come to mistrust the world -- especially the social world.

THE BABY'S SOCIAL PREDISPOSITION

As the baby acquires more advanced motor, cognitive, and social skills the quality of the mother-infant interaction changes.

Communicating with the Baby:

One important way that adults communicate with infants is through facial expressions. Adults tend to exaggerate their facial expressions and vocalizations when communicating with infants. They also employ **"motherese,"** in a high pitch and volume which is punctuated with great variations in sound level. Infants can discriminate between many affective expressions and appear to prefer positive emotions.

The Baby Communicates:

The infant is capable of expressing him- or herself through gestures, gaze, and sound and facial expressions. Crying is a powerful tool for communicating because it has a strong immediate effect on those around them. The infant's ability to make eye contact is an important milestone in social development. It vastly increases the infant's responsivity and serves to fuel the joint interaction.

The Infant's Emotional Life:

Psychologists have been interested in the origins and developmental course of emotions such as joy, fear and surprise since 1872, with the publication of Darwin's The Expression of Emotions in Man and Animals. In the past decade, several new directions in the study of emotions have emerged. In the 1930's Katherine Bridges conducted classic observational studies of infants' emotions. She theorized that babies are born with just one basic emotional reaction, **generalized excitement**, that differentiates with development. The first step in differentiation is to a general positive affect (delight) and a general negative affect (distress). Subsequently emotions such as disgust, fear, anger and affection emerge. Other researchers, like Carol Izard, argue that while we do not know what infants feel inside, they are capable of a range of emotional expressions similar to those of adults.

Smiling:

For parents, the baby's smile is a sign that they are appreciated and loved. There are three stages of smiling in the first year. For the first weeks of life the infant's smile is considered **endogenous**, or internally triggered. During this time, babies smile most during states of irregular sleep and drowsiness when there is increased brain activity, which suggests a biological component to the smile. Next to emerge, at 3-5 weeks, is the **nonselective social smile**, which is exogenous or externally triggered but which appears in response to a variety of rhythmic or repetitive events (e.g., a nodding head, blinking lights). The nonselective smile is most easily elicited by a human face or the mother's voice. This smile becomes increasingly social and instrumental and at about five to six months of age the **selective social smile** appears. This smile is directed toward familiar individuals. There is clearly a social component to the emergence of smiling as well as a biological component because babies who do not receive adequate social interaction will smile later than babies raised in socially stimulating environments.

Theories of Smiling:

The **evolutionary theory of smiling** emphasizes the smile's adaptive value; the smile makes it more likely that the infant will receive parental attention and affection. **Cognitive theorists** recognize that the smile is a means of social communication, but they emphasize the cognitive bases of the infant's social behavior and emotional expressions. They contend that the smile is an expression of intense pleasure following the mastery of a cognitive task.

Fear:

Children display different fears depending on their age. For example, toddlers associate fear with pain (e.g., a doctor may remind them of a painful injection). In preschool, children are afraid of monsters, animals, and the dark (some of which they have not experienced directly). During the middle childhood years children begin to fear failing in school or with peers. The fears which children evidence are in part a function of their cognitive capacities.

Fear of Strangers and Separation Anxiety:

Stranger anxiety (the infant's negative response to an unfamiliar adult) and **separation anxiety** (the infant's negative response to the impending or actual leave taking of an attachment figure) are especially evident in the latter half of the first year of life (five or six months to 13 months). Whether or not an infant will express stranger anxiety is mediated by the mother's response to the stranger. If the mother is friendly toward the stranger, the negative display will be less intense than if the mother is neutral or negative in her interactions with the stranger. Social referencing refers to the infant's looking to adults in the environment to make use of social cues (i.e., the parent's affective expressions) to guide his or her own emotional response. Psychoanalysts suggest that stranger anxiety is related to the baby's love for the mother and the fear of losing her. Ethologists suggest it is a response to an intuitive appraisal of a potentially dangerous situation. Cognitive theorists suggest stranger anxiety arises because the infant is unable to assimilate the stranger's face into their existing schema. Separation anxiety has been understood as related to the cognitive phenomenon of object permanence. The baby can now represent or think about the mother while she is gone, but does not have the cognitive capacity to understand where she has gone or that she will return. Prior to achieving object permanence, the infant does not represent or recall the absent mother and therefore does not miss her.

ESTABLISHING RELATIONSHIPS

Attachment:

Separation anxiety is also one indicator of the infant's attachment to his or her primary caregiver. Researchers define the attachment relationship, one of the most important socialization experiences, as a strong and enduring bond that develops between the infant and the person he or she most frequently interacts with. This attachment results in a feeling of emotional security. As most of the research is conducted with mothers, the focus of the discussion is on mothers. However, there are many important attachment relationships in an infant's world (e.g., fathers, siblings, grandparents, childcare providers). Researchers have studied specific infant behaviors to operationalize the attachment relationship. These behaviors include: the extent to which an infant looks toward the mother, smiles at her, orients his body toward her, maintains physical proximity, and becomes upset upon separation. Mary Ainsworth, who was strongly influenced by John Bowlby, identified several phases in the attachment process: 1) preattachment, a period in which the infant does not discriminate among people and can be soothed by a stranger (first weeks of life); 2) differential response to familiar and unfamiliar people (3 months); 3) strong preference for primary caretaker (beginning around 6-8 months and peaking at 1 year).

Individual Differences in Attachment:

Ainsworth developed a laboratory procedure, called the **Strange Situation**, to study individual differences in attachment. This involves seven episodes including the introduction of a strange adult and several brief separations from the mother. Observing the infant's behavior in these episodes, and paying special attention to how the infant responds to the final reunion with the mother, Ainsworth and her colleagues classified infants in terms of the security of their attachment relationship. The groups include **secure**, **anxious**, and **avoidant**. These individual differences in the laboratory correspond to differences in mother and infant behaviors at home.

Learning theorists hypothesized that infants became attached to their mothers through repeated associations of experiencing their mothers as a source of relief from discomfort and pain. John Bowlby, who was influenced by ethology, psychoanalytic theory, and Piagetian theory, viewed attachment as a unique response serving to protect the young from harm and conceptualized the attachment relationship in terms of a **behavioral system** which serves to keep the infant in the proximity of the caregiver.

Influences on Attachment:

Infants differ in the quality of the attachment relationship, the age at which attachment behaviors emerge, and the number of people they are attached to. There is a transaction between caregiver sensitivity (which is in part a function of social support to the caregiver) and infant characteristics in the development of attachment relationships.

Cultural Influences on Attachment:

By studying parenting and attachment relationships across cultures, notable differences have been found in rates of attachment which appear to be associated with culturally held beliefs about parenting.

Importance of Attachment:

Through interactions with the caregiver, the infant acquires security and a sense of trust in ability of the caregiver to provide for the infant's needs. This sense of security is connected to the infant's ability to explore her surroundings and learn from them and to later social relationships (e.g., peer relationships). The mother becomes a **secure base** from which the infant can venture forth into the world and to which the infant can return for nurturance and refueling.

Maternal Deprivation and Separation:

The study of infants who are deprived of the opportunity to form an attachment relationship has contributed to our understanding of the importance of the

81

attachment relationship and implications for later development. Harlow's studies with infant monkeys illustrates the significance of the infant's interaction with the mother. Monkeys raised with surrogate wire or cloth "mothers" displayed bizarre social and exploratory behaviors in later life. Similarly, monkey infants raised only with peer monkeys exhibited significant problems, spending a majority of their time clinging to one another. Studies of human infants raised in institutions which provide physical care but inadequate social stimulation grow up with intellectual deficits and social impairments. Infants raised in institutions which offer both physical and social stimulation as well as individual attention from a limited number of caregivers do not evidence these kinds of difficulties. However, in addition to receiving appropriate stimulation, infants require consistency and continuity of care. Frequent changes or disruptions in the caregiver - child relationships disrupt the ability to form an appropriate attachment relationship. Although infants can and do withstand brief separations (e.g., birth of a sibling, parent's work or vacation travel), long-term separations are difficult for them to cope with.

Discussion of Social Issues: Foster Care:

The foster care system was established to meet children's needs when their parents' behavior constitutes a serious risk for the children as when a parent physically or sexually abuses the child or fails to meet basic needs (e.g., food, shelter, education). In these cases social agencies may intervene, at times removing the child from the home and placing him in a foster home. Although this is meant to be a temporary measure, a majority of children remain in foster care for two or more years, and some remain in foster care for their entire childhood. A problem with the design of our foster care system is that it is crisis oriented rather than preventive. Sending a home visitor to support and enhance the skills of a family who is at-risk for a child being placed out of home before the child is in imminent danger might eliminate the need for removal and enhance the child's long-term social and emotional development. In response to the importance of consistency and continuity of care, the foster care system has been modified to increase the likelihood that children in the foster care system will have a permanent living situation (i.e., by making more children eligible for adoption).

Infants of Working Mothers:

As mentioned earlier, there is little consensus on the impact of infant out-of-home care in the first year of life. This is in part due to the lack of well-conceived, longitudinal studies. Others have questioned the measures employed in these studies. For example, the strange situation is often the critical measure of attachment. However, since children in out-of-home care are exposed to more separations and more strangers than children who are cared for by a parent in the home, this may not be an appropriate measure. When infants of mothers employed out-of-home are found to have less secure attachments than infants of mothers working in their homes, findings can also be interpreted to reflect the greater level of stress in the out-of-home families. For example, in some studies, mothers working out-of-home were more likely to be single than mothers working in-home.

Parental-Leave Policies:

Because out-of-home care for infants is the sole option available to many working couples and single parents, some developmental psychologists and policy makers have advocated a national parental leave policy to care for a newborn baby, a newly adopted child, or a child who is ill.

Infants and Their Fathers:

Father-infant relationships have been a neglected topic of study until fairly recently. However, available studies indicate that infants do form an attachment relationship with their fathers. Important differences characterize father-infant interactions from those with mothers. First, more interactions occur in the context of play and these play interactions tend to be highly arousing and more physical. While roles for men and women are changing in the family, women in the U.S. continue to take primary responsibility for their infant's care. Inclusion of the father in infancy research is critical as it can provide a window into the family system and the marital relationship.

Peer Relations:

    As increasing numbers of infants are placed in group
care settings, there has been renewed interest in the
study of young infants' peer relations. Recent studies
suggest that infants are interested in and respond to other
infants. Even at birth, they respond to other neonates'
cries more than to older children. Peer relations appear
to follow a developmental sequence. Infants younger than
three months look at one another. Three- to four-month-
old infants touch and six-month-old infants smile at one
another. As infants become mobile, they approach and
follow their age-mates. True social exchanges begin at
approximately 12 months. Initially, infants will
independently focus on a shared object. Slightly older
infants will play contingency games (one child acts and
the other responds). Finally, at 20 months of age,
infants begin a stage of complementary interchanges and
turn taking.

KEY TERMS AND CONCEPTS

Complete each sentence with the best word or phrase. Check your answers against the key at the end of this chapter.

1. Infants who are distressed by the presence of strangers are often said to be experiencing _____.

2. When infants consider the response of a trusted adult before responding themselves to a novel situation, they are engaging in _____.

3. The laboratory procedure in which an infant's responses to separations and reunions with her mother are assessed is the _____.

4. The Eriksonian crisis of infancy is _____.

5. A national _____ law would permit parents to spend more time with their newborns without jeopardizing their employment status.

6. The capacity of mothers and infants to modify one another's behavior is called _____.

7. Katharine Bridges proposed that the newborn's only emotion was _____.

8. The bond that emerges over time between parent and child is called _____.

9. Klaus and Kennel originally proposed that mother-infant _____ could only occur in the moments immediately following delivery.

10. Rene Spitz's most influential work involved the emotional development of _____ infants.

MATCHING EXERCISE

Match each name to the idea, research field, or accomplishment associated with it. Answers are in the Answer Key at the end of the chapter.

1. Daniel Stern   a. blind infants

2. Erik Erikson   b. 1930s' work on infant
                               emotion

3. Selma Fraiberg   c. Strange Situation

4. Charles Darwin   d. infant-mother attunement

5. Katharine Bridges   e. trust vs. mistrust

6. Jean Piaget   f. maternal deprivation

7. Mary Ainsworth   g. cognitive theories of
                               smiling

8. John Bowlby   h. comparative studies of
                               attachment

9. Harry Harlowe   i. 1st work on development of
                               emotional expression
10. Rene Spitz
                           j. attachment as a behavioral
                               system

MULTIPLE CHOICE SELF-TEST

_____1.   Erikson described the crisis represented by infancy as
   a.   isolation vs. intimacy
   b.   trust vs. mistrust
   c.   autonomy vs. shame
   d.   initiative vs. guilt

_____2.   The infant's vision is best adapted to focus on objects which are _____ away.
   a.   12"
   b.   2"
   c.   6'
   d.   12'

_____3.   Selma Fraiberg is remembered for her work with _____ infants.
   a.   deaf
   b.   blind
   c.   paralyzed
   d.   mentally retarded

_____4.   The infant's preference for the mother emerges at about
   a.   birth
   b.   6 weeks
   c.   3 months
   d.   6 months

_____5.   The work of Harlowe, Spitz, Ainsworth, and others points to
   a.   the need for continuity of care
   b.   the handicapped infant's ability to relate to others
   c.   the need for open adoptions
   d.   available mechanisms for government subsidy of child care

_____6. Women are entering the work force in greater
numbers than ever because
a. more fathers are assuming child care
responsibilities
b. of economic need
c. the School of the 21st Century provides
universal day care
d. a wider range of child care options permits
them to

_____7. The infant's use of another person's behavior
in interpreting a novel situation is called
a. stranger awareness
b. attachment
c. social referencing
d. reciprocity

_____8. Infants tend to smile longer at
a. complex visual stimuli
b. solid yellow objects
c. simple visual stimuli
d. solid white objects

_____9. Harry Harlowe's research heavily influenced
concepts of
a. initiative vs. guilt
b. attachment
c. positive reinforcement
d. operant conditioning

_____10. Fathers are _____mothers
a. less competent caregivers than
b. more competent caregivers than
c. different caregivers than
d. totally inadequate caregivers compared with

RECOMMENDATIONS FOR FURTHER READING

Biringen, Z., & Robinson, J. (1991). Emotional availability in mother-child interactions: A reconceptualization for research. American Journal of Orthopsychiatry, 61, 258-271.

Bornstein, M. H., & Bruner, J. S. (1989). Interaction in Human Development. Hillsdale, NJ: Lawrence Erlbaum Associates.

Bornstein, M. H., Tamis-LeMonda, C. S., Pecheux, M. G., & Rahn, C. W. (1991). Mother and infant activity and interaction in France and the United States: A comparative study. International Journal of Behavioral Development, 14, 21-43.

Brazelton, T. B. (1985). Infants and Mothers. New York: Delta.

Field, T. (1990). Infancy. Cambridge, MA: Harvard University Press.

Greenspan, S. I., & Pollock, G. H. (1989). The Course of Life: Vol. II: Early Childhood. Madison, CT: International Universities Press.

Stern, D. (1985). The Interpersonal World of the Infant. New York: Basic Books.

Vaughn, B. E., & Waters, E. (1990). Attachment behavior at home and in the laboratory: Q-sort observations and Strange Situation classifications of one-year-olds. Child Development, 61, 1965-1973.

ANSWER KEY FOR SELF-TEST ITEMS

Key Terms and Concepts

1. stranger anxiety (or stranger awareness)
2. social referencing
3. Strange Situation procedure (or Strange Situation paradigm)
4. trust vs. mistrust
5. infant (or parental) care
6. reciprocity
7. generalized excitement
8. attachment
9. bonding
10. institutionalized

Matching

1-d; 2-e; 3-a; 4-i; 5-b; 6-g; 7-c; 8-j; 9-h; 10-f

Multiple Choice

1.	b	6.	b
2.	a	7.	c
3.	b	8.	a
4.	d	9.	b
5.	a	10.	c

CHAPTER 8

PHYSICAL DEVELOPMENT IN THE PRESCHOOL PERIOD

STUDY GOALS

In studying Chapter 8, you should arrive at an understanding of the following topics and issues:

1. The physical changes that characterize the preschool child, and how these are influenced by nutrition, health care, and psychosocial factors.

2. Brain development and lateralization, and its implications for motor skills and language acquisition.

3. The status of child health care in the United States, and how it compares with health care delivery systems in other nations.

4. The leading causes of death among U.S. preschoolers, and what is---and isn't---being done to improve outcomes for these children.

CHAPTER OVERVIEW

PROGRESS IN PHYSICAL GROWTH AND MOTOR DEVELOPMENT

Physical Growth:

   Weight, Height, and Changes in Body Proportions.
Growth in weight and height occur at a much slower rate in the preschool years as compared to infancy. Between ages two and six, the average North American child gains only four to five pounds per year and grows approximately 3 inches per year. Thus, the average 6-year-old weighs 45 pounds and is 43 inches high. Children often eat less during the preschool years than they did in infancy. Later, in adolescence, as growth once again assumes a fast pace, there is an increase in appetite. The changes in weight and height are less significant than changes in body proportions. Toddlers (ages 2-3 years) still have protruding stomachs, swaybacks, bent legs, and relatively

large heads which are characteristic of infancy. In the preschool years the child will begin to appear taller, straighter and thinner, resulting in a decrease in the ratio of head size to body size.

Skeletal Maturity. During the preschool years the child's bones become longer, thicker, and harder. Specifically, **ossification**, the process whereby cartilage is gradually replaced by bone, occurs at a rapid rate during the preschool years. Using an X-ray of a child's hand to evaluate the child's rate of ossification relative to norms, physicians determine **bone age** (or skeletal age).

Brain Development. By the time a child is five years old, the brain attains 90 percent of its adult weight. Weight gains during the preschool years reflect an increase in the size of neurons due to **myelination**, a process whereby a fatty substance forms a sheath around nerve fibers. At the same time there is an increase in the size of **glial cells** which support the nerve cells. The brain is organized into right and left hemispheres which each contain "centers" that control different abilities and functions. The left hemisphere is primarily responsible for receiving, processing, and producing language. The right hemisphere is primarily responsible for processing spatial information, either visual or tactile, and visual imagery. Thus, the left hemisphere primarily codes input in terms of **linguistic descriptions**, whereas the right hemisphere codes images. Through **lateralization**, a dominant hemisphere attains increasing control over certain functions (e.g., writing). Lateralization is now believed to begin in the first months of life. Most often, both sides of the brain work together and where an injury destroys part of one hemisphere, the other hemisphere can sometimes fill in. There is greater **plasticity of the brain** (or ability for regions to assume functions typically controlled by other regions) prior to early adolescence.

Implications for Language Acquisition. Maturation of the centers responsible for language skills is associated with **myelogenetic cycles**, during which myelination occurs to particular functional centers within the brain. According to Lecours, there are three myelogenetic cycles associated with the child's increased language ability. The first involves the brainstem and is associated with sound production. The second is related to the acquisition of language skills during the preschool years. The third, involving the upper cortex, is not complete until adolescence.

   <u>Implications for Motor Development</u>. Myelination of nerve fibers which control voluntary movement is complete at approximately age three to four. This appears to be associated with the preschooler's ability to master fine motor skills (e.g., writing with a pencil, tying shoe laces).

The Development of Motor Skills:

   Increases in height and brain development enable the preschooler to experiment with a variety of movements and to acquire and refine both **gross motor** (large muscle) and **fine motor** (muscles of hands and fingers) skills. This proficiency emerges primarily in the context of play. Gross motor skills typically are mastered prior to fine motor skills. Children's developing fine motor skills and the integration of these skills with advances in cognition can be appreciated through their art work. Kellogg describes four stages of the preschooler's art: 1) **placement stage** or scribbling; 2) **shape stage** at approximately age three, during which they create geometric shapes (e.g., circles); 3) **design stage** at approximately three and a half to four and a half, combining shapes; and 4) **pictorial stage**, as the drawings increasingly represent important people and objects in their world. There is currently some concern that children, and especially children in child care, are not engaging in gross motor physical activities on a daily basis.

   <u>Sex Differences and Similarities</u>. On average, boys tend to be more muscular than girls, lose their baby fat sooner than girls, and have less body fat throughout the life span. In contrast, girls mature more rapidly in bone ossification, and certain functional centers in the brain mature earlier. Boys tend to be better in motor skills such as catching and throwing while girls evidence an advantage in fine motor skills such as writing and drawing, as well as gross motor activities which require coordination and balance rather than strength (e.g., skipping). However, at this age there is considerable overlap in the two distributions.

Increased Competence in Self-Help Skills:

   Toilet Training. Toilet training is a developmental
milestone attained during the early part of the preschool
period, usually by the time a child is three. Toilet
training appears to be dependent on cultural norms, as
some societies achieve toilet training during the first
year of life. Parents should realize that toilet
training is a process and long after a child has been
trained, accidents can occur when the child is unduly
stressed or tired.

INFLUENCES ON GROWTH

   Individual differences in growth are a function of
genetic factors and differences in nutrition and health
care.

Malnutrition:

   There is a close relationship between nutrition and
the child's growth and development. Protein-energy
undernutrition, a condition known to limit growth and
development, affects an estimated 40-60 percent of
children worldwide. This condition has deleterious
effects on the central nervous system and interferes with
the development of adaptive and intellectual capacities
in children, especially if it coincides with a critical
period for brain growth. Many U.S. children, especially
among the poor, go to bed hungry and are at risk for this
as well as other nutritional disorders (e.g., anemia, or
iron deficiency). Approximately one in eight youngsters
under age 12 in the U.S. lives in a household where there
is not enough to eat. Undernutrition can also affect
attention and memory processes, behavior, and a reduced
capacity to fight infectious diseases. Undernutrition in
the preschool years limits skeletal development,
resulting in short stature. A moderate degree of
malnutrition for a brief time may be overcome when the
nutritional deficits are corrected.

   Emotional Factors. Recovery from undernutrition
depends partly on physical factors and partly on
emotional factors. Because malnourished children are
less socially responsive, their parents may not interact
with them often, facilitating their continued withdrawal

and lack of responsivity. Supportive interventions may
be necessary to break this cycle once food supplements
are administered. In a disorder known as **failure to thrive**
(when onset is in infancy) or **deprivation dwarfism**, a
child may receive adequate nutrition but fails to grow
because he is subjected to emotional abuse and/or
neglect. This emotional situation inhibits the secretion
of adequate amounts of growth hormone. Failure to thrive
may have physiologic roots, such as a digestive disorder.
When physiologic factors cannot be found or do not fully
account for the infant's appearance, emotional factors
are suspected. With deprivation dwarfism there is often
a complex and sustaining relationship between parental
attitude and children's behavior.

Obesity:

    At the opposite end of the spectrum is **obesity** (an
excess of body weight), which also has physical and
psychological problems associated with it. Obesity is
associated with an increased risk of high blood pressure,
gall bladder disease, and adult onset diabetes. In
addition, obese children are often teased or socially
isolated by peers. There is strong evidence that
genetics plays a role in obesity. However, the number of
young children who are not necessarily obese but are
overweight appears to be increasing due to a greater
reliance on processed food, snacking, and T.V. viewing
which contributes to a more sedentary life-style.

    <u>Lack of Physical Fitness</u>. American children as a
group are exceedingly sedentary by world standards. A
sedentary life-style can affect general health in
addition to weight.   Over the past ten years, the
federal government has reduced the amount of money spent
for physical education.

Health Care:

    It is critical to provide all children access to
medical care. The preschool child is especially
vulnerable to respiratory infections and childhood
illnesses (German measles, mumps). These diseases do not
cause any discernible growth slowdown as long as the
child is well nourished and receives adequate medical
attention. However, even a seemingly minor medical

problem, like an ear infection, can cause deafness and/or language difficulties if untreated. In addition, many medical illnesses can be prevented through immunization.

Child Health Care in the U.S. Increased spending on children's health in the 1960s and 1970s as well as programs such as Head Start have expanded the number of children's health services and caused a substantial decline in the number of children who become ill. However, many children in this country have not shared equally in this health improvement. There are sharp disparities based on family income. Poor children are more likely to be exposed to lead, to suffer nutritional deficits, and to be exposed prenatally to drugs and the AIDS virus. Also, reduction (beginning in the 1980s) in public funds for children's services has also affected health services. The Medicaid program is one of the ways the U.S. attempts to insure health care for poor children. However, its implementation varies from state to state, with some states adhering to much stricter income-eligibility requirements than others. As a result, only two-fifths of the poor children in this country are covered by this program. As poor health is linked to classroom failure, school absenteeism, and children's misconduct in the streets, the lack of adequate health care services should be of great concern to students of developmental psychology.

Child Health Care in Other Countries. Williams and Miller (1991) looked at children's health conditions in 10 European countries. They found that all these countries had better infant and child survival rates than the U.S. and found that more children in the U.S. died of injuries. Further, the U.S. lagged behind many countries in immunizing children. In all 10 countries, health services are financed under national systems assuring services to all children in part by requiring them to be registered with a health provider at birth; and nearly all European children are enrolled by age three or four in public preschools that are linked with health care programs. In the U.S., children are not required to be registered until age 6 for enrollment in elementary school.

Childhood Injury Prevention. Injuries are the leading cause of death among children ages 1 to 14. Many of these deaths are preventable, as injuries occur in highly predictable patterns. Motor vehicle-related injuries account for over half of the deaths due to injuries. For preschoolers, however, home-related injuries are most prevalent (e.g., fires, scalding, falls, drowning, choking, and to a lesser degree poisoning).

Preventing Injuries to Children. Educational programs designed to teach parents about reducing household hazards should be one component of a national agenda aimed at preventing injuries to children. Some research suggests that parents are most responsive to educational intervention in the prenatal stage of development. In addition to educational efforts, some injury-control specialists suggest that automatic safety features should be required (e.g., automatic safety restraints in automobiles). There are legal implications to legislating parental compliance with safety practices. For example, some states prosecute parents when their child dies in an automobile accident if the child was not wearing a seatbelt.

KEY TERMS AND CONCEPTS

Complete the following sentences by inserting the most appropriate word or phrase; correct answers appear at the end of the chapter.

1. Replacement of cartilage by bone is called _____.

2. Obesity is determined by measuring _____.

3. The brain is divided into two _____.

4. The left hemisphere of the brain controls the _____ side of the body.

5. The process through which one hemisphere of the brain becomes dominant is called _____.

6. A child whose weight is below the 3rd percentile for his or her age is said to suffer from _____.

7. The two types of motor skills are _____ and _____.

8. _____ of all American preschoolers are not adequately immunized against childhood disease.

9. Motor skill proficiency is best practiced by preschoolers in the context of _____.

10. By age 5, the brain has achieved _____% of its adult weight.

MULTIPLE CHOICE SELF-TEST

_____1.   By age 2, the child's brain has reached
           _____% of its adult weight.
      a.   25
      b.   50
      c.   75
      d.   100

_____2.   Ossification is completed by
      a.   the 2nd trimester of pregnancy
      b.   birth
      c.   late adolescence
      d.   middle age

_____3.   _____ input is encoded in the left
           half of the brain; _____ input on the
           right side.
      a.   linguistic; mathematical
      b.   linguistic; image
      c.   image; linguistic
      d.   image; emotional

_____4.   The process through which a protective fatty
           coating is deposited on nerve fibers is
      a.   myelination
      b.   lateralization
      c.   ossification
      d.   failure to thrive

_____5.   The leading cause of death among U.S. children
           between 1 and 14 is
      a.   pediatric AIDS
      b.   measles
      c.   heart disease
      d.   injuries

_____6.   Measles and whooping cough
      a.   are now found only in developing nations
      b.   are on the decline
      c.   are on the rise again
      d.   have been completely eradicated

_____ 7. The left hemisphere of the brain controls
a. the left side of the body
b. the right side of the body
c. the back of the body
d. the front of the body

_____ 8. The most significant bodily change in the preschool years is a change in
a. weight
b. height
c. head circumference
d. body proportions

_____ 9. The development of motor skills depends on
a. brain development and practice
b. maturation alone
c. experience alone
d. nutrition alone

_____ 10. The pictorial stage of children's art occurs at about age
a. 1 or 2
b. 2 or 3
c. 4 or 5
d. 11 or 12

RECOMMENDATIONS FOR FURTHER READING

Carter, A.S., & Sparrow, S.S. (1989). The acquisition of adaptive behavior in infancy: Developmentally at-risk infants. Seminars in Perinatology, 13, 474-481.

Cicchetti, D., & Carlson, V. (Eds.) (1989). Child Maltreatment: Theories and Research on the Causes and Consequences of Child Abuse and Neglect. New York: Cambridge University Press.

Cleveland, W. W. (1991). Redoing the health care quilt: Patches or whole cloth? American Journal of Diseases of Children, 145, 499-504.

Haggarty, M. S. (1991). Pediatric acquired immunodeficiency syndrome, poverty, and national priorities. American Journal of Diseases of Childhood, 145, 527-528.

Kaufman, J., & Zigler, E. (1987). Do abused children become abusive parents? American Journal of Orthopsychiatry, 57, 186-192.

Oseid, S., & Carlsen, S. (1989). Children and exercise XIII. Champaign, IL: Human Kinetics Books.

ANSWER KEY FOR SELF-TEST ITEMS

Key Terms and Concepts

1. ossification
2. skinfold thickness
3. hemispheres
4. right
5. lateralization
6. failure to thrive
7. gross; fine
8. one-third
9. play
10. 90

Multiple Choice

1. c
2. c
3. b
4. a
5. d

6. c
7. b
8. d
9. a
10. c

CHAPTER 9

COGNITIVE AND LANGUAGE DEVELOPMENT DURING
THE PRESCHOOL YEARS

STUDY GOALS

After studying Chapter 9, you should have a good grasp of
the following areas and issues.

1. Piagetian theory of cognitive development as it
applies to children of preschool age, including all
relevant terms and concepts. How the preschool child
differs cognitively from infants and toddlers.

2. Alternatives to a Piagetian approach, including the
neo-Piagetian, information processing, and cultural
context orientations. How these draw upon and differ
from Piaget's work and ideas.

3. The basic linguistic milestones of the preschool
period, and rules governing these. The relationship
between language and thought according to Vygotsky,
Bruner, and others.

4. The major influences on learning in the preschool
child, and how these factors interact. Preschool,
television, the family, and the child care environment
should be considered.

5. The rationale behind, mechanisms for and
effectiveness of intervention strategies aimed at
preschoolers.

CHAPTER OVERVIEW

Piaget's Theory:

   The Preoperational Period. Children at this stage
of Piagetian development have advanced beyond the
restrictions of a sensorimotor level of cognitive
development but have not yet attained the kinds of skills
necessary for thinking logically. Recent researchers
suggest that Piaget may have underestimated the cognitive

capabilities of preschoolers. Piaget explained that as the young child practices his ability for representational thought, he acquires a symbolic mode of thinking, or symbolic functioning. This refers to the child's ability to mentally represent, or use symbols to create, an object which is not present. Some symbolic representations are fairly concrete (e.g., image of a hammer) while others are more abstract (e.g., letters h-a-m-m-e-r). Piaget termed highly abstract mental representations signs and believed these emerged after more concrete representations. Piaget argued that three skills emerge which reflect symbolic mediation: **deferred imitation** (e.g., dancing like Grover on Sesame Street), **symbolic play** (e.g., pretending to feed a doll), and sophisticated language skills.

The Development of Concepts. A concept is a way of organizing information so that it is applicable not only to a specific object or event but to other similar objects and events. The acquisition of concepts greatly simplifies learning. Recent research suggests that during the sensorimotor period children acquire very simple, or concrete, concepts (e.g., shape). However, more abstract concpets (e.g., numbers) are acquired slowly and are not fully attained until the school-aged years. During the preoperational period the child appears to be confused between a class of objects and its subclasses, and centers on only a single dimension at a time. In addition, the preschool child is easily fooled by appearances because he lacks an understanding of **the concept of conservation**, that an amount remains the same even though the shape may change. Thus, the child centers on the change in shape, the dimension which is salient for the preschooler, and loses track of the amount remaining stable. For this reason, preschoolers have difficulty distinguishing between appearance and reality. Piaget also characterized preschool thinking in terms of **irreversibility** of thought, which refers to the inability of the child to go forward and then backward in his thinking (e.g., remembering and incorporating what was just seen into what is currently visible).

Practical Applications. The preschool child uses **transductive reasoning**, which refers to the process of going from one particular to another particular, often ascribing cause and effect connections to unrelated events (e.g., the sidewalk is blamed for a fall). This is often confusing to parents, who think the child is being silly or manipulative.

Egocentrism refers to the child's tendency to interpret the environment from her own point of view. Often a child will attribute blame to the self in situations which are not associated with the child's behavior (e.g., death, divorce). Piaget also described a related phenomenon, **perspective taking**, and argued that preschoolers also have difficulty taking the perspective of the other. More recently, investigators have argued that the tasks Piaget employed to address this issue were too abstract and have found that when Piaget's tasks are simplified, three-year-olds are capable of taking the perspective of the other. A real-life example of preschool perspective taking is when four-year-olds modify their speech patterns (i.e., use baby talk, shorter utterances) so that infants and very young children they are playing with can better understand them.

The Search for Alternative Explanations of Cognition:

Neo-Piagetian Approach. Some neo-Piagetian researchers maintain the view that cognitive skills appear in a stepwise fashion, but argue that they are more domain-specific than Piaget thought. We perform best in domains we are most familiar with.

An Emphasis on the Cultural Context:

Some researchers emphasize the influence of social environment on cognition, noting that adults create a context that supports the child's learning of different behaviors.

Information Processing. Information processing researchers reinterpret Piaget's findings in terms of preschoolers' limited capacity to process information. **Limited attention span** limits the level of detail which is processed and increases the likelihood of errors. **Limited memory capacities** also constrain information processing. Memory for specific events, referred to as **autobiographical memory**, begins by age three and increases with age. Preschoolers do not employ strategies to try to remember (e.g., repeating things, or grouping similar events or objects). Instead, they remember events that make a strong impression.

LANGUAGE DEVELOPMENT

Learning Words and Speaking in Sentences:

During the preschool years the child acquires the ability to speak in longer sentences (and paragraphs!), to use complex sentences and to have a command of the tenses. Along with a rapid increase in vocabulary, some preschoolers will develop an idiolect, or idiosyncratic but generally communicative vocabulary or language structure (e.g., stocks to refer to socks and stockings). In addition, while a child may use and understand words in specific contexts, their cognitive limitations may prevent a more abstract understanding or use of the word.

Learning the Rules of Grammar:

Grammatical rules such as word order and word form enhance the communicative advantage of words. The use of a preferential looking pattern paradigm, in which children view two video-tapes simultaneously while listening to words or sentences, has aided researchers studying the syntactic comprehension of infants as young as one year of age. Gradual grammatical progress is evident in preschoolers' use of questions and negatives (e.g., "Mommy?" becomes "Where is my mommy?" and "No take" becomes "Don't take this"). While there are large individual differences among children in terms of the rate of acquiring vocabulary and grammatical forms, there is consistency in the order in which many dimensions of language are acquired. For example, the order in which children acquire **morphemes**, or qualifiers (e.g., ing, ed, s), is the same for most children. In addition, children are learning general rules which they can apply in novel situations.

Overregularization. While preschoolers' use of grammatical rules clearly enhances the acquisition of language structure and form, it also leads to systematic errors associated with **overregularization**. When children first learn a new grammatical rule they tend to apply it to all words, including words which they previously used correctly (e.g., "went" switches to "goed" as they overemploy the "ed" past tense rule).

<u>Learning the Meaning of Words</u>. Researchers propose that preschoolers are biased, or predisposed to assign meaning to new words according to specific principles of learning. For example, the **principle of uniqueness**, or the **no-synonym rule**, states that for every new word there is a new meaning. The first label children learn is interpreted by them to refer to the basic level of meaning. All other words referring to the object are interpreted as describing characteristics of the object. **Articulation**, the ability to pronounce words correctly, often lags behind vocabulary. In some cases, articulation difficulties are a function of immature motor control. Common errors include dropping the first consonants of some words (e.g., spoon is pronounced "poon"), or difficulty articulating the "th" sound (e.g., thick is pronounced "fick").

Egocentric and Socialized Speech:

During the preschool period speech becomes increasingly social. Piaget characterized speech as **egocentric**, which refers to children carrying on a monologue or focusing speech on their own needs, or **socialized**, which refers to the communication of thoughts, intentions, and desires to others. Socialized speech is also characterized by the child's increased ability to take the perspective of the other which facilitates the exchange of information between speaker and listener.

Learning to Communicate:

Effective communication involves three skills: 1) the ability to engage the listener's attention; 2) the ability to speak in a way the listener understands; and 3) the ability to listen. A vast majority of preschoolers are quite capable of using verbal and non-verbal cues to attract the listener's attention. However, the preschool child is developing capacities which will influence speaking to the specific audience and listening, important aspects of social speech. These skills include perspective taking and decentration.

Language and Thought:

For adults, language and thought are so indistinguishable that thinking often seems like talking

or communicating with oneself. However, with children,
there is considerable debate about whether children must
first have the words in order to develop the thought, or
whether they first have the thought and find the words.
Piaget argued that since language reflects thought it
cannot precede cognitive development. Thus, language
does not structure thought; rather it is the vehicle for
expressing it. From studying preschoolers' inability to
describe their own behavior (e.g., crawling), he argued
that although preschoolers have the motor capacity and
the vocabulary, they do not acquire the cognitive skills
necessary to understand and explain their behavior until
later in the preschool years. In contrast, Lev
Vygotsky, a Russian psychologist, contended that language
is an instrument of thought that comes to regulate the
child's thoughts, planning strategies and behavior. For
example, Vygotsky argued that what Piaget termed
egocentric speech serves a specific function: to
regulate the child's behavior and thinking (i.e., provide
the child with self-management skills). Initially, this
process is external (i.e., the child gives self-
directives out loud). Over time, however, this self-
regulation is internalized. Some researchers contend
that while children initially learn language, language
does facilitate learning. Language is also a primary
tool provided by culture for acquiring information about
the world view of a given culture.

The Learning Environments of the Young Child:

    The Family. By paying attention to the young child
and sharing daily discoveries, concerns, successes and
failures, parents can enhance the child's sense of
curiosity and inclination to learn from experience.
Reading to children, talking to children, listening to
children, playing games (both with rules and pretend),
and going on outings (e.g., supermarket, neighbor's
house, zoo, library, or park) are all activities which
enhance cognitive development. Researchers consistently
report that the quality of family life (e.g., parental
attentivenesss and availability of playthings) is
strongly related to the child's cognitive development.

    Child Care. In general, research sugests that
children who are participating in well-run, good-quality
child care centers are not at a developmental disadvantage
compared to children who spend most of their time at

home. Good quality day care centers may even benefit some children who come from homes that do not provide opportunities for reading, manipulating objects, and playing with peers. More research is needed which addresses the influence of adequate child care centers and the many other child care arrangements that are commonly used (e.g., family child care, relative care).

Choosing/Evaluating Child Care:

Caretakers with training in early childhood education and child development spend more time with each child, and are more likely to comfort, praise, and provide guidance than caretakers without such training. Frequent verbal interaction between caretakers and children appears to be a key determinant of quality because it facilitates language acquisition and social-emotional development. A good-quality child care center should: 1) employ a sufficient number of staff to ensure that children are supervised at all times and there is ample opportunity for interaction (staff:child ratio of 1:3 for infants, no more than 12 children per class for three-year-olds and 16 for four-year-olds); 2) provide a safe yet stimulating environment (i.e., many materials to manipulate); and 3) provide stability or consistency of care (i.e., low staff turnover rates). Finally, it is in the best interest of the child that parents and child care staff form a close working relationship. Thus, **parent involvement** is another critical dimension of quality care.

Television. Most homes have at least two television sets. Researchers estimate that children spend between 11 and 28 hours viewing each week and all agree that children spend more time watching television than in any other activity except sleep. While many parents are concerned about the level of violence and aggression children view on television, it is also clear that television can be an effective teaching method for communicating prosocial content. These programs are also cost effective, reaching vast numbers of children simultaneously. Parents can help children acquire benefits from T.V. viewing by watching with them and talking about the program. This parent mediation may be especially important for preschoolers because they still have difficulty distinguishing reality from fantasy.

<u>Preschool</u>. Children who are not enrolled in child care are often enrolled in a preschool program several mornings a week. Preschool programs, often designed to prepare children for kindergarten and first grade, provide the child with an opportunity to play with same-aged peers and with a variety of play materials, and teach children about following a routine (e.g., circle time for sharing, reading a book, free play or activity choice time, snack, art activity, outside time, etc.).

Discussion of Social Issues: Preschool Intervention Programs:

Many children enter school without the prerequisite skills for learning in the school environment. Such children, most often from poor homes, fail in school and therefore do not acquire the skills needed to succeed in society. In the 1960s, as part of the War on Poverty, emphasis was placed on providing preschool education for disadvantaged children. **Project Head Start** is one of the country's best-known early intervention programs. Having existed for 25 years, Project Head Start is now a family of 2,000 programs which vary in the quality and types of services offered (e.g., center-based vs. home-based). Despite the differences there are some common assumptions which underlie all of the Project Head Start programs: 1) Respect for varied backgrounds and deemphasis of deficits; 2) inclusion of parents in planning and administration; 3) focus on children's health and nutrition; 4) inclusion of researchers to facilitate the goal of accumulating basic knowledge regarding processes which can enhance and inhibit development.

Evaluation of Early Intervention Programs:

Initially researchers used only IQ tests to determine whether or not children benefitted from Project Head Start programs. They neglected the benefits experienced by other family members (e.g., parents and siblings) and the health and social-emotional benefits experienced by children in the program. The early research which was limited to IQ outcomes demonstrated that children's IQ scores did improve in the program, but later "faded out." Using a broader model of evaluation, recent evaluations demonstrate that children who have participated in Project Head Start perform better in school and in their personal lives than those who do not.

Preschool education is quite cost effective for society. Indeed, for every $1 spent on preschool intervention programs, society can save approximately $4.75 in costs for remedial education, welfare, and crime down the road.

Renewed Interest in School Readiness:

From educators to the president, there is consensus on the need to promote "school readiness." This consensus is to some extent a result of the outcome evaluations discussed above.

School Readiness: What Does It Mean?

Current efforts to ensure children's success in school are addressing the needs of families from pregnancy through infancy and into the preschool years. Assaults to development in utero can result in a wide range of developmental problems that will limit the child's learning capacities. Further, programs for infants and toddlers facilitate early identification of developmental problems.

KEY TERMS AND CONCEPTS

Fill in the blank with the most fitting word or group of words. Then see the Answer Key at the end of the chapter to check your responses.

1. A _____ is a way of organizing information so that it is applicable not only to a specific object or event but to other similar objects and events as well.

2. Piaget called the abstract symbol used to represent an object a _____.

3. A child's idiosyncratic but communicative use of language is that child's _____.

4. Piaget characterized the speech of young children as being either egocentric or _____.

5. _____ functioning refers to the child's ability to understand, create, and use symbols to represent something that is not present.

6. The concept of _____ involves the understanding that matter retains its quantity even when shaped or arranged differently.

7. A child engaged in _____ reasoning often ascribes cause and effect relationships to unrelated events.

8. The preschool years correspond to the Piagetian _____ period.

9. Word qualifiers such as the suffixes -ed and -ing are known as _____.

10. An important component of good quality child care is a high _____.

MATCHING EXERCISE

1. Jean Piaget   a. domain specific cognitive development

2. Neo-Piagetians   b. child care standards

3. Lev Vygotsky   c. language as a cultural tool

4. Joseph McVicker Hunt   d. preoperational thought

5. Noam Chomsky   e. adolescent learning

6. Reuven Feuerstein   f. innate linguistic structures

7. Jerome Bruner   g. environment and intelligence

8. National Day Care   h. language and thought
   Study

_____ 1. Joseph McVicker Hunt emphasized the role of
_____ in determining IQ.
a. maturation
b. ethnicity
c. the environment
d. heritability

_____ 2. A child who uses a doll to represent a baby is
engaging in
a. symbolic play
b. conservation
c. formal operational thought
d. egocentrism

_____ 3. The child who says "pat doggie" to indicate her
desire to pat the dog is using
a. egocentric speech
b. centering
c. transductive reasoning
d. telegraphic speech

_____ 4. The child's need for structure is a central
focus of
a. Montessori schools
b. private preschools
d. family day care
d. center-based day care

_____ 5. Who argued that language acquisition and
comprehension are aided by innate cognitive
structures?
a. Jean Piaget
b. Lev Vygotsky
c. Noam Chomsky
d. Joseph McVicker Hunt

_____ 6. Reuven Feuerstein is known for his research on
a. the effect of stimulus deprivation in rats
b. educational interventions for adolescents
c. language acquisition during the preschool
period
d. neo-Piagetian perspectives on creativity

_____ 7. Head Start was developed to
a. enhance social competence and overall functioning
b. raise IQ by 10-20 points
c. prevent juvenile delinquency
d. promote a multicultural view of history

_____ 8. Absolute size of a day care grouping is
a. irrelevant, as long as there are enough caregivers
b. something that has yet to be studied
c. a crucial component of child care quality
d. only important in obtaining licensing

_____ 9. Other than sleep, what single activity occupies the greatest percentage of the preschool child's time?
a. eating
b. playing outdoors
c. attending nursery school
d. watching television

_____ 10. According to Piaget, the preschool child is in the _____ stage.
a. phallic
b. sensorimotor
c. preoperational
d. operational

RECOMMENDATIONS FOR FURTHER READING

Bringuier, C. (1980). Conversations With Jean Piaget. Chicago: University of Chicago Press.

Ginsberg, H. P., & Opper, S. (1988). Piaget's Theory of Intellectual Development. Englewood Cliffs: Prentice-Hall.

Markman, E. M. (1989). Categorization and naming in children: Problems of induction. Cambridge, MA: MIT Press.

Miller, S. (1988). Parents' beliefs about children's cognitive development. Child Development, 59, 259-285.

National Association for the Education of Young Children (1988). Position statement on standardized testing of young children 3-8 years of age. Young Children, March.

Piaget, J. (1967). Language and Thought of the Child. Chicago: University of Chicago Press.

Piaget, J. (1977). The Essential Piaget. New York: Basic Books.

Piaget, J. (1985). The Equilibration of Cognitive Structures: The Central Problem of Intellectual Development. Chicago: University of Chicago Press.

Tobin, J. (1989). Preschool in Three Cultures: Japan, China and the United States. New Haven: Yale University Press.

Vygotskii, L. (1986). Language and Thought. Cambridge, MA: MIT Press.

ANSWER KEY FOR SELF-TEST ITEMS

Key Terms and Concepts

1. concept
2. sign
3. idiolect
4. socialized
5. symbolic
6. conservation
7. transductive
8. preoperational
9. morphemes
10. staff:child ratio

Matching

1-d; 2-a; 3-h; 4-g; 5-f; 6-e; 7-c; 8-b

Multiple Choice

1.	c	6.	b
2.	a	7.	a
3.	d	8.	c
4.	a	9.	d
5.	c	10.	c

CHAPTER 10

SOCIAL AND EMOTIONAL DEVELOPMENT

DURING THE PRESCHOOL YEARS

STUDY GOALS

After studying Chapter 10, you should be able to:

1. Describe the most salient aspects of the social and emotional development of the preschool child, including interaction with family members, peers, and other caregivers. Describe how earlier stages of development lay the framework for this stage. Describe the development and importance of play. What enables the young child to play? What does play enable the young child to do?

2. Explain the nature and origins of aggression from a variety of theoretical perspectives.

3. Explain the emergence of and influences on sex differences in behavior. Grasp the difference between gender role and gender identity. Describe a number of theoretical perspectives on sex differences, including, but not limited to, the psychoanalytic point of view and learning theory's approach to this issue.

4. Detail some of the factors that influence the socialization of the preschool child, including the effects of child care, television, parenting styles, and family.

CHAPTER OVERVIEW

THE SOCIAL WORLD OF THE PRESCHOOL CHILD

Expanding Family Relations:

The changes in the preschooler's social world occur in the context of the child's increased independence and developmental strides in cognition and physical development. Many preschoolers, having achieved a

secure, warm and trusting relationship, are ready to
explore the environment beyond the immediate family, and
develop close relations with other adults and peers.

Interaction with Mother. The preschool child is
still very closely linked with her primary caregiver, or
psychological parent. She will frequently check to see
where her parent is and will play independently for a
longer period of time when she knows where her parent is
or can hear her parent's voice. While increasingly able
to tolerate separations from the parent (e.g., to attend
nursery school or a friend's house), under periods of
stress difficulty with separation is not uncommon. The
preschooler's parents are beginning to have higher
expectations for self-reliance and independence.

Interactions with the Father. Research with fathers
in two-parent families where mothers are the primary
caregivers suggests that these fathers become
increasingly involved in parenting. They are more likely
to spend time playing with and disciplining their
children. Preschoolers begin to differentiate unique
characteristics of their parents and will direct their
behavior to the parent most likely to reinforce them.
For example, preschool children, and especially boys,
appear to prefer the father as a playmate.

Discussion of Social Issues: Children of Divorce:

Due to increased rates of divorce and women bearing
children outside of marriage, many children are living in
single-parent families. In the early 1980s, one-fifth of
children under the age of five were living in single-
parent families, 90 percent of which were headed by
women. A majority of men and women who divorce will
remarry, and the marriages involve a series of
transitions and household reorganizations that children
have to adjust to. For children in single-parent
households, the absence of a second parent often means
there is less social, emotional, and financial support.
All of the tasks and responsibilities of parenting are
shouldered by one individual. Also, many fathers become
emotionally detached from their children following a
divorce. Another issue affecting many children of
divorce is failure to provide adequate **child support**
payments, the monetary payment made by the parent who
does not have custody of the child to the parent with

custody. Aside from the direct effects of divorce, the familial conflict that preceded the divorce may place children at increased risk for emotional difficulties. Preschool children experience a great deal of stress at the divorce of their parents because they have difficulty understanding the divorce and due to egocentrism take responsibility for the divorce. However, the negative impact of divorce is not inevitable. How well the child adjusts to the divorce is mediated by the quality of the parents' post-divorce relationship and the availability of social supports.

Relations with Siblings:

Researchers have tended to focus on the negative aspects of sibling relations, noting that **sibling rivalry**, the conflict between brothers and sisters, is common. In addition to aggressive interactions, siblings also cooperate and act affectionately toward one another.

Peer Relations:

Friends and Friendships. Preschoolers spend increasing amounts of time with other children and the child's interest in and involvement with other children are expanding. Having a friend and being someone's friend are very important to preschool children.

The Value of Peer Relationships. Relationships with peers provide emotional support, facilitate the development of social skills, and provide a means for preschool children to compare themselves to others their own age.

Play:

Types of Play. Peers are also partners in play. Garvey (1977) defined **play** as any pleasurable, spontaneous, and voluntary activity that is an end to itself and has no extrinsic goal. Consistent with this, Hughes (1991) stated that play has several essential elements: it is intrinsically motivated, freely chosen, pleasurable, and actively engaged in by participants. There are many forms of play in the preschool period including:

Solitary Play, where the child is playing alone with a toy or another object;

Parallel Play, where children play by themselves but they are close to another child and often playing with similar toys or objects;

Associative Play, where children borrow and lend toys, talk about the same activity, or follow one another, but there is no attempt to organize a group activity; and

Cooperative Play, where several children play in an activity that engages all those in the group; and in which the children have a shared goal.

Influences on Play. As children grow older, they become more sociable in their play patterns. In addition to age, **experience** with peers and the **opportunity** for play (i.e., space and materials) influence the quality of preschool play.

Dramatic Play. Make-believe or pretend play begins at approximately age two when the child is capable of symbolic representations. Initially, the play is solitary. After age three, children engage in make-believe play in cooperation with other children and by the time they are four or five they engage in **sociodramatic play**, which is make-believe play about social situations (e.g., family). Sociodramatic play provides opportunities for learning about adult roles and helps them to understand real life experiences.

Relating to Others:

There are striking differences in children's personality characteristics which are a function of the complex interplay between heredity and environment.

Aggression. The expression of **aggression** becomes evident in the preschool years. Patterson (1982) proposed a **performance theory** of childhood aggression, noting that aggressive and other maladaptive behaviors are learned, shaped, and maintained by forces operating in the social setting. More recently, the role of the child's contributions to social interactions has been emphasized, noting that some children are more likely to provoke physical punishment than others.

<u>Altruism and Empathy</u>. **Altruism** is an aspect of moral behavior involving a concern for the welfare of others. **Altruistic behavior** is a voluntary and intentional action that benefits others and is not motivated by any desire to obtain external rewards. A three-year-old who offers a toy to a crying child is evidencing altruistic behavior. Such acts of altruism require **empathy**, the ability to experience the feelings of another person. Prosocial behaviors are facilitated when children see adults behaving in prosocial ways. However, offering an **explicit reward** (e.g., a new toy) does not promote prosocial behavior.

The Emergence of Self-Concept:

With age, children acquire a subjective understanding and evaluation of their own personality, qualities, and capabilities. These impressions about oneself are based on the individual's own interpretation of experiences in the social and physical world and on the feedback received from others. Preschoolers typically define themselves in relatively specific and concrete terms (e.g., by name), or in terms of frequent activities or behaviors ("I run fast"). Evidence of a self-concept begins in the second year of life as toddlers begin to recognize themselves in the mirror and in pictures, and to use linguistic terms such as "me" or "mine." <u>Gender Identity</u> refers to the child's awareness and acceptance of being either a boy or girl. Most children can distinguish between males and females by two years of age and by two and a half can answer the question, "Are you a girl or a boy?" Stability of gender identity, or knowing that one's gender will not change, is established later in the preschool years and is associated with the Piagetian concept of reversibility. <u>Gender Role</u>. During the preschool years children also learn socially prescribed **gender roles**, or socially defined behaviors and attitudes associated with being a male or a female. **Androgynous** is a term that is used to describe an individual who combines feminine and masculine characteristics. **Undifferentiated** is a term which describes an individual who does not behave in an especially feminine or masculine way. These latter two terms are useful given the changing gender roles in our society. Researchers have found that preschoolers are often very rigid in adopting sex-role sterotypic behavior. From ages 4 to 7 children are increasingly likely to believe that certain activities or tasks are restricted to one sex or the other. This suggests that they adopt not only sex-typed behaviors but sex-typed attitudes as well.

Explaining Sex Differences in Behavior:

Sex differences in behavior continue to be evident throughout life.

Biological Factors. Many current studies attempting to find a link between biology and sex differences in behavior focus on hormones, in part due to the association between testosterone and aggression. Because males and females are socialized differently from birth, it is very difficult to attribute differences in behavior to biology alone.

Environmental Factors. Studies of situations in which children were born with ambiguous genitals and parents and professionals assign a sex and raise the child accordingly highlight the importance of environmental influence on the acquisition of gender roles and the child's awareness of gender. Parents' Role. The child learns about the behavioral differences between the sexes from the behavior of those around him (e.g., parents, siblings, peers, teachers) and from other sources (e.g, books and T.V.). Not only do children learn about differences between males and females from observing their parents' behavior, parents have different expectations from their sons and daughters and treat them in ways which promote sex-stereotypical functioning. Boys are more likely to be encouraged to be competitive and independent while girls are more likely to be encouraged to be nurturant and emotionally expressive. Fathers appear to play a central role for boys and girls.

Cross-Cultural Perspective. Cross-cultural studies highlight the varying roles played by girls and boys in different cultures and the manner in which these roles influence behavior (e.g., where girls care for younger siblings they are more nurturant).
The Psychoanalytic Theory. Psychoanalytic theorists contend that the adoption of sex-typed attitudes and behaviors is the result of **identification**, a process whereby the child unconsciously adopts another's attitudes and behaviors as their own. Freud described

the boy's identification with the father resulting from the resolution of the **Oedipus conflict** (i.e., pushing out of consciousness the wish to be with the mother because fear of retaliation by the father -- or castration anxiety). In a somewhat similar vein, Freud described the girl's identification with the mother resulting from the resolution of the **Electra conflict**, (i.e., penis envy) as a function of pushing out of consciousness the wish to be with the father because of fear of resentment of the mother.

Learning Theory. Social learning theorists state that children acquire all behavior, including gender roles, through the mechanisms of **reinforcement** and **punishment**. Observational theorists emphasize that children do not need to be reinforced directly. They learn through observation and imitate their parents as well as other socializers (siblings, teachers, T.V. personalities).

Cognitive-Developmental Theory. Elaborating the role of imitation, cognitive-developmental theorists emphasize that an awareness of gender precedes any attempt by the child to imitate the behaviors of the same-sex people he encounters. Children actively seek out same-sex models to imitate because they value others who are like themselves. Bem's **gender schema theory** suggests that a schema is a series of ideas that help the child organize information and adapt his or her behavior accordingly.

SOCIALIZATION

Socialization refers to the process whereby members of one generation shape the behavior and personality of members of the younger generation so that children come to behave in socially acceptable ways. The precise behaviors needed to behave in different societies differ.

Socialization in the Family. The family is the core socialization agency. During the preschool years the main attributes of socialization are **self-control, social judgment** and **prosocial behaviors**. The young child must learn to regulate his or her behavior (e.g, wait for a turn), assess social situations, form internal standards of conduct, and adopt positively valued behaviors.

123

<u>Parental Care-Giving Practices</u>. Parents continually
teach the child to behave in socially appropriate ways,
both setting limits on inappropriate and prompting
appropriate behaviors. However, there are many parenting
styles which appear to relate to children's development.
Three central styles were identified by Baumrind:

> 1) **Authoritarian Parents**, who require the
> child to accept the adult's word and authority,
> are likely to favor punitive and forceful
> disciplinary measures when a child's behavior
> comes into conflict with parental standards,
> and are likely to be controlling and cold in
> interactions with children. Children of
> authoritarian parents are more likely to be
> moody, apprehensive, and vulnerable to stress;
> 2) **Permissive Parents**, who allow the child to
> govern her own behavior, attempt to interact
> with the child in a non-punitive and accepting
> manner, and are likely to be warm and friendly
> in interactions. Children of permissive
> parents appear cheerful, but have little self-
> reliance, are frequently out of control, and
> have difficulty inhibiting their impulses;
> 3) **Authoritative Parents** are the most
> nurturant and effective. They use positive
> reinforcement along with reprimands and
> punishment to guide their children's behavior;
> when punishment is used, they explain the
> rationale behind their disciplinary actions.
> In addition, they are warm in interactions and
> encourage independence. Children of
> authoritative parents are cheerful, friendly,
> and socially adept.

<u>Effective Discipline Techniques</u>. The most effective
discipline strategies foster self-regulation and social
judgment in the child without detracting from her
initiative and self-confidence and without generating
excessive compliance or rebellion. Positive methods of
discipline recognize the importance of clear rules that
are understood by the child and reinforce prosocial and
appropriate behaviors. When, however, punishment is
necessary, the method of discipline should be instructive
and directed toward the child's negative behaviors rather
than at the child's worth as a person. Furthermore, in
order for punishment to be effective, **timing** and

124

consistency are critical. The longer the delay between the initiation act and the onset of punishment, the less effective the punishment. Many researchers argue that physical punishment should be avoided. Physical punishment serves as a model of aggression that the child is likely to imitate, increasing aggression and teaching that physical aggression is a viable way to solve interpersonal disputes.

Minority Group Children in the United States:

There are many ethnic groups within the United States that have unique systems of beliefs and practices regarding child-rearing. Developmental psychologists are recognizing the importance of studying minority children within their cultural and familial context and the need to emphasize the strengths associated with being a minority group child. For example, in several ethnic groups the availability of an extended family network, which promotes **interdependence** as a goal of socialization, leads to increased cooperation in contrast to competition.

The Role of Television:

Television Violence. Television devotes a significant amount of time to violence and aggression. For example, crime is portrayed 10 times more often on the screen than it occurs in real life. Studies have documented that exposure to T.V. violence increases aggressive acts.

Television and Prosocial Behaviors. Programs such as "Mr. Rogers' Neighborhood" can lead to increased self-control and reduced aggression.

Television and Minorities. Television producers have begun offering a diversity of programs featuring minorities in a positive light (e.g., "The Cosby Show").

Effects of Child Care on Socialization. Children in full-time child care centers are more cooperative in their interactions with peers than are children who are raised at home. However, these characteristics are mediated by the quality of care in the child care centers.

KEY TERMS AND CONCEPTS

Fill in each blank with the best word or phrase. Answers can be found at the end of this chapter.

1. When young children play near but not actually <u>with</u> one another, they are engaging in _____ play.

2. Aggressive behavior is shaped and maintained by social forces. This is a tenet of the _____ theory of aggression.

3. The Oedipus conflict is successfully resolved through and results in _____ with the same-sex parent.

4. Having a realistic sense of, and accepting, one's own gender is defined as gender _____.

5. Engaging in culturally sanctioned behaviors associated with one's own gender is sex _____.

6. _____ is intentionally behaving in a way that benefits others without a desire to obtain personal rewards.

7. That learning can be reinforced by affection, approval, and praise is an idea central to _____ theory.

8. According to Baumrind, _____ parents are controlling, forceful, and punitive.

9. The most nurturant and effective parenting style is _____.

10. According to Freud, aggression is a _____.

MATCHING EXERCISE

1.	Furstenberg	a.	performance theory
2.	Bandura	b.	learning theory
3.	Patterson	c.	minorities in the media
4.	Piaget	d.	autonomy vs. shame
5.	Bem	e.	children of divorce
6.	Gutierrez	f.	gender schema theory
7.	Clarke-Stewart	g.	day care and socialization
8.	Erikson	h.	egocentrism of preschool child
9.	Baumrind	i.	moral development
10.	Kohlberg	j.	parenting styles

MULTIPLE CHOICE SELF-TEST

_____1. According to Freud, aggression
   a. only arises after resolution of the Oedipal crises
   b. is a biological instinct
   c. is learned from watching one's parents
   d. is shaped by forces in the social setting

_____2. Susan Harter's research indicates that children 2 to 3 years of age
   a. are already capable of empathy
   b. are too egocentric to be empathetic
   c. display empathy if rewarded
   d. display empathy only toward peers

_____3. Gender identification is typically established by age
   a. 3
   b. 5
   c. 2 in girls, 4 in boys
   d. 8

_____4. The behavior of fathers affects the socialization of
a. sons only
b. daughters only
c. sons and daughters
d. all children, but only as mediated by the mother

_____5. Discipline is
a. unnecessary in well-run homes
b. most effective when consistent and instructive
c. often best achieved through spanking
d. against the law in Sweden

_____6. The quality of the staff in a child care setting
a. doesn't matter much as long as high staff:child ratios are maintained
b. hasn't yet been studied
c. isn't important enough to pay extra for
d. is the most important factor in day care's effects on socialization

_____7. Erikson posited that the central tension during the preschool years results from conflict between
a. trust vs. mistrust
b. male and female gender identity
c. autonomy vs. shame and initiative vs. guilt
d. industry vs. inferiority

_____8. Noncustodial fathers, a year after divorce,
a. rarely see their children
b. often spend more time with their children than before the divorce
c. spend less time with daughters, more time with sons
d. usually re-petition the court for custody

_____9. The most well-adjusted children are those whose parents' style is
a. authoritarian
b. permissive
c. authoritative
d. eclectic

_____10.　　Gender identity is
　　　a.　　another term for gender role
　　　b.　　another term for sex role
　　　c.　　defined by the behaviors in which the child
　　　　　　engages
　　　d.　　the child's confidence in and comfort with his
　　　　　　or her gender

RECOMMENDATIONS FOR FURTHER READING

Bretherton, I., & Watson, M. W. (1990).　Children's perspectives on the family.　New Directions for Child Development, No. 48.　San Francisco:　Jossey-Bass.

Campbell, S. B. (1990).　Behavior problems in preschool children.　New York:　Guilford Press.

Damon, W., & Hart, D. (1988).　Self-Understanding in Childhood and Adolescence.　New York:　Cambridge University Press.

Dornbusch, S. M., & Strober, M. H. (1988).　Feminism, Children, and the New Families.　New York:　Guilford Press.

Kelly-Byrne, D. (1989).　A Child's Play Life.　New York: Teachers College Press.

Lyytinen, P. (1991).　Developmental trends in children's pretend play.　Child Care, Health, and Development, 17, 9-25.

McGuire, J., & Earls, F. (1991).　Prevention of psychiatric disorders in early childhoood.　Journal of Child Psychology and Psychiatry and Allied Disciplines, 32, 129-153.

Rescorla, L., Parker, R., & Stolley, P. (1991).　Ability, achievement, and adjustment in homeless children. American Journal of Orthopsychiatry, 61, 210-222.

Reznick, J. S., Kagan, J., Snidman, N., Gersten, M., Baak, K., & Rosenberg, A. (1986).　Inhibited and uninhibited children:　A followup study.　Child Development, 57, 660-680.

ANSWER KEY FOR SELF-TEST ITEMS

Key Terms and Concepts

1. parallel
2. performance
3. identification
4. identity
5. stereotyping
6. altruism
7. social learning
8. authoritarian
9. authoritative
10. biological instinct

Matching

1-e; 2-b; 3-a; 4-h; 5-f; 6-c; 7-g; 8-d; 9-j;
10-i

Multiple Choice

1.	b	6.	d
2.	a	7.	c
3.	a	8.	b
4.	c	9.	c
5.	b	10.	d

CHAPTER 11

PHYSICAL DEVELOPMENT DURING MIDDLE CHILDHOOD

STUDY GOALS

After studying Chapter 11, you should be familiar with:

1. The typical path of growth and development in the school-aged child, and individual variations in such growth. Historical trends in physical maturation and how to interpret them at the level of the individual child.

2. Physically based variations in growth and behavior, such as attention deficit disorders and extreme variations in physical stature. The origin and treatment of such variations in growth and behavior and the social/ethical issues raised by such treatment.

3. Obstacles to optimal child health, including obesity, stress, injury, and lack of access to appropriate health care.

CHAPTER OVERVIEW

Progress in Physical Growth and Motor Development

Motor Skills:

Physical development during the school-aged years is characterized by steady and sustained growth and the maturation of higher cortical functions in the brain. There are also advances in the ability to execute motor skills and master more complex and elaborate motor tasks. When studying physical development in the school-aged years, the principles important for early physical development are quite relevant. In addition, physical growth and motor development begin to assume great personal significance. As children acquire the ability to think about what others think, others' reactions become more important. Further, there is great variability among children of the same age in height and rate of maturation. Secular trend is a term which refers to changes in physical growth over time. There is a

secular trend for all children to mature at an earlier age.

Motor Skills:

There is marked improvement in fine motor skills which leads to enjoyment and mastery in a variety of activities (e.g., writing, playing a musical instrument, sewing, detailed drawing). Similarly, there is improvement in gross motor skills, as evidenced by greater speed, power, balance, agility, and coordination. Many children are interested in participating in team sports such as soccer, baseball, and basketball or learning and mastering complex tasks such as dancing, swimming, roller skating or playing tennis.

Sex Differences and Similarities. While differences in motor skills between boys and girls are minimal during this phase of development, boys continue to have greater strength and girls have greater coordination and balance.

Physical Growth:

Physical growth in the school-aged years proceeds at a slow but even pace.

Individual Differences. There are many individual differences in motor skills including competency and activity level.

Hyperactive and Hypoactive Children. Differences may be accentuated by the school setting, where children are often required to sit still and attend to specific tasks for long periods of time. While previously referred to as suffering from **hyperactive syndrome** or **minimal brain dysfunction** (MBD), children who are inattentive, impulsive, and/or hyperactive are currently labeled with the terms **Attention Deficit Disorder** (ADD) or **Attention Deficit Hyperactivity Disorder** (ADHD). ADHD is a relatively common disorder which occurs more frequently among boys than among girls. In addition to increased risk for learning difficulties, these children are often disliked by their peers. Attentional problems often persist into adolescence and adulthood (e.g., antisocial behavior, marital difficulties, traffic accidents). There is considerable controversy regarding the etiology of ADHD. In addition, there is controversy surrounding

132

the treatment of the disorder. Ritalin, a stimulant medication, appears to produce moderate to dramatic improvements in the behavior of about 75 percent of ADHD children. However, there are some side effects, including interfering with physical growth and overuse. Behavior modification and providing increased structure in the classroom can also facilitate the child's ability to learn and become involved in social activities.

Variations in Growth. Children differ in body build and in rates of growth. Rate of growth is influenced by genetic endowment, nutrition, and physical and emotional health. There is a secular trend for stature (height), such that the average height has increased over the last several generations.

Implications for Psychological Development. Variations in height are rarely a source of concern from a medical point of view. However, being too tall or too short can be a source of embarrassment during the middle school years. Given the emphasis on peer relations and the propensity of some children to tease or reject children who are somewhat different, being very tall or short can sometimes lead to negative feelings about oneself and, more specifically, a negative self-image. Individuals who are teased as children are more likely to 1) be dissatisfied with their bodies, 2) be depressed, and 3) have low self-esteem. Concerns with body image are quite common among school-aged children, and especially common among girls.

HEALTH ISSUES

Obesity:

Obesity is becoming increasingly common among children and can have serious implications for physical and mental health. A significant portion of some children's caloric intake is "junk food." This can interfere with adequate nutrition. In addition, obesity places children at increased risk for high blood pressure, which is associated with later heart disease.

Stress:

Stress was defined by Selye (1983) as "wear and

tear" on the body which results from the extreme
physiological changes the body undergoes in response to
novel and negative experiences. When the body maintains
a stress response over a long period of time, the body
may become weakened and vulnerable to disease. While
childhood is often thought of as a happy and protected
time, in reality, children are exposed to a wide range of
stressors. These include: changes in family life (e.g.,
divorce), high expectations or pressure to succeed, and
exposure to violence. Physical effects of stress on
children can range from mild to severe and include:
stomachaches, sleep disturbances, headaches, chronic
infections, and susceptibility to illness. Changes in
societal structure have also reduced social supports
available to children to buffer the impact of these
stressors.

Injuries:

Injuries are the greatest cause of death and
disability in childhood. The types of injuries children
sustain differ by age: Toddlers and preschool children
are at risk for suffocation, house fires, falls, and
drowning; children ages 5 to 9 suffer the highest number
of pedestrian injuries; and among children ages 10 to 14,
injuries sustained while riding a bicycle are prevalent.
These differences are in part a function of parents'
allowing children increasing independence (e.g., crossing
streets alone). Educational programs aimed at parents
and school children may reduce the number of injuries in
this age group (e.g., prevention strategies emphasizing
bicycle helmets). Legislative initiative may also be
warranted due to the limited effectiveness of some
educational efforts.

Health Care:

With the exception of obesity, stress and injuries,
most children do not experience any major health problems
during the school-age years. For the most part, children
have correctable dental and visual problems along with
minor illnesses. Approximately 10-15 percent have
chronic illnesses, which last at least three months and
require extensive hospitalization or in-home services
(e.g., leukemia, migraine headaches, severe asthma).
Schools are obligated by law to provide education to
these children in the least restrictive setting possible.

However, many school systems are not well equipped to manage medically involved children and therefore provide in-home tutors.

Discussion of Social Issues: Homeless Children:

Another group of children requiring special health attention at school are homeless children. Families with children make up the fastest growing segment of the homeless population. Family life for homeless children is characterized by instability and discontinuity which places the child at risk for various emotional difficulties (depression, anxiety, sleep disturbances, abnormal fears, aggression control). School performance, nutrition, and health are also problematic.

KEY TERMS AND CONCEPTS

Fill in the blanks with the word or phrase that best completes the sentence.

1. _____ describes the way in which maturation occurs at earlier ages in successive generations.

2. The childhood disease responsible for the most missed days of school is _____.

3. Restlessness, distractibility, chaotic behavior, and lack of appropriate inhibitions are symptoms of _____.

4. _____ refers to the overall functioning of the cardiovascular system.

5. Children with attentional disorders whose behavior is characterized by low activity levels and daydreaming are said to be _____.

6. The drug Ritalin is commonly used to treat _____.

7. The onset of puberty in girls is defined by _____, or the appearance of the first menstrual period.

8. A Center for Disease Control study indicates that by age 11, _____% of young girls are already dieting.

9. The most common cause of death in middle childhood is _____.

10. Hans Selye is best known for his research on _____.

MULTIPLE CHOICE SELF-TEST

_____1.   Menarche is
        a.   the beginning of puberty in girls
        b.   the beginning of puberty in boys and girls
        c.   occurring later in each generation
        d.   a necessary precursor to sexual activity

_____2.   ADD and ADHD are _____ times more likely in
             boys than girls.
        a.   20
        b.   2
        c.   4
        d.   100

_____3.   Ritalin is commonly used in the treatment of
        a.   LD
        b.   ADHD
        c.   PKU
        d.   growth deficits

_____4.   During the middle childhood years, children
        a.   display a natural inclination to be active
        b.   display a natural tendency to be passive
        c.   prefer sedentary activities
        d.   should be discouraged from overexertion

_____ 5. By middle childhood, temperament observed in
          infancy
    a.   has been replaced by new styles of behavior
    b.   persists and may even be accentuated
    c.   can no longer be measured
    d.   has become irrelevant

_____ 6. Daydreaming, passivity, and poor attention are
          characteristics of
    a.   MBD
    b.   ADD
    c.   ADHD
    d.   hypoactivity

_____ 7. Feingold's work on ADHD focuses on
    a.   the efficacy of psychotherapy as treatment
    b.   the heritability of ADHD
    c.   elimination of food additives
    d.   use of behavior modification techniques

_____ 8. Secular trends in height
    a.   are decreasing with every generation
    b.   are beginning to level off
    c.   can not be demonstrated after the 1940s
    d.   are changing only among females

_____ 9. Eating disorders are
    a.   strictly an adolescent phenomenon
    b.   on the decline among American youth
    c.   harmless variations in dieting behavior
    d.   becoming more prevalent among school children

_____ 10. The velocity of growth increases from birth
          until
    a.   age 3
    b.   age 6
    c.   puberty
    d.   adulthood

RECOMMENDATIONS FOR FURTHER READING

Hewlett, S. A. (1991). When the Bough Breaks: The Cost of Neglecting Our Children. New York: Basic Books.

Hinman, A. R. (1991). What will it take to fully protect all American children with vaccines? American Journal of Diseases of Children, 145, 559-564.

Johnston, R. B. (1991). Poverty and the health of American children: Implications for academic pediatrics. American Journal of Diseases of Children, 145, 507-509.

Krugman, R. D. (1991). Child abuse and neglect: Critical first steps in response to a national emergency: The report of the U.S. Advisory Board on Child Abuse and Neglect. American Journal of Diseases of Children, 145, 513-515.

Parker, R. M., Rescorla, L. A., Finkelstein, J. A., Barnes, N. B., Holmes, J. H., & Stolley, P. D. (1991). A survey of the health of homeless children in Philadelphia shelters. American Journal of Diseases of Children, 145, 520-526.

ANSWER KEY FOR SELF-TEST ITEMS

Key Terms and Concepts

1. secular trend
2. asthma
3. Attention Deficit Disorder (or Attention Deficit Hyperactivity Disorder)
4. Physical fitness
5. hypoactive
6. ADHD
7. menarche
8. 50
9. injury
10. stress

Multiple Choice

1. a
2. c
3. b
4. a
5. b

6. d
7. c
8. b
9. d
10. c

CHAPTER 12

COGNITIVE DEVELOPMENT DURING MIDDLE CHILDHOOD

STUDY GOALS

A thorough reading of Chapter 12 should leave you with a basic understanding of:

1. The major approaches to cognition during middle childhood. How children at this stage differ from preschool children in their thinking, and what limitations persist at this stage.

2. How language development continues to progress, and how formal education and television affect this development. What educational strategies are most effective in promoting linguistic competence in a variety of different educational situations.

3. How problems in learning can emerge, and what factors influence the development and resolution of learning difficulties.

CHAPTER OVERVIEW

Information-Processing Approach:

   During middle childhood the ability to encode, store, and retrieve information from the environment through basic processes such as attention and memory improves dramatically.

Attention:

   Selective attention refers to the process whereby we focus on relevant stimuli in the environment and ignore irrelevant stimuli. With age, children are increasingly able to attend to relevant stimuli, are less easily distracted by irrelevant stimuli, more flexible in shifting attention from one stimulus to another, and able to attend for longer periods of time.

Memory:

Drawing upon a store of memories from past experiences enhances learning because the child can use previous strategies to solve problems and acquire new knowledge. Storing information involves three storage systems: sensory memory, short-term memory, and long-term memory. Some researchers use the term **working memory** to refer to short-term memory. Others suggest that short-term memory refers to performance on tasks testing for memory relatively soon after the person acquires the information while working memory represents the information we are attending to at a given time.

Memory-Aiding Devices or **Mnemonic strategies** are often employed by school-aged children to facilitate memory. For example, **rehearsal** is repeating information over and over to facilitate memory. School-age children may also use **organization**, or grouping items to be remembered into meaningful clusters of information (e.g., foods, toys, animals) and **external aids** (e.g., writing something down).

Metamemory is an intuitive understanding or self-awareness about how memory works. The older the child, the more aware he or she is of the limitation in memory capacity and the more likely they will realize that a strategy will be necessary to commit something to memory.

Accumulating Knowledge, or an increased knowledge base, facilitates memory because it is easier to remember things that are familiar. This is especially true for children.

PIAGET'S THEORY

The Concrete Operations Period:

Piaget explained that there are **qualitative** changes that occur between 7 to 12 years of age in terms of greater flexibility of thought and the ability to think logically. In addition, the child is now able to perform **mental operations.** Mental operations refer to the ability to mentally transform, modify, or otherwise manipulate what is seen and heard according to logical rules (e.g., reversibility, which is the ability to perform mental inversions, or to mentally undo a sequence of actions). Thus, the school-age child is said to be **operational**. However, the child is only capable of performing mental operations on concrete and tangible objects or on signs of these objects. Hence, Piaget called this the **concrete operations period**. The most important aspect of operational thought is the ability to perform mental inversions, which Piaget termed **reversibility**. A related operational ability is **decentering**, the ability to focus on more than one feature of an object at a time (e.g., color and shape). In addition, children develop the capacity to recognize that a change in one feature can be balanced by an equal and opposite change in another, referred to as **reciprocity**.

<u>Conservation</u> refers to the ability to recognize that two equal quantities remain equal even if we change one in some way (e.g., shape) as long as nothing is added or removed. Piaget devised several tasks which allowed him to study the emergence of concrete thinking (e.g., pouring liquid into a container of a different shape, rolling a ball of clay into a sausage shape). Through these tasks and careful inquiries he described three stages of concrete thinking: First, children will believe and state that one of the two objects is bigger. Next, they will give the correct answer but will not be able to provide an explanation and may change their minds when the change is repeated or reversed. Finally, at approximately age seven, children can follow and remember transformations and can provide an explanation for why the two objects are the same even though an irrelevant feature has been changed.

<u>Unevenness of Development</u>. Children do not acquire conservation of all properties at the same time but there is consistency across children in the order properties are acquired: first number, then length, liquid quantity, mass, area, weight, and finally volume. Piaget termed this variability **horizontal decalage**, to explain why a child may have all the reasoning necessary to solve the problem but because the concept is more difficult it emerges later in development. In part this is due to lack of familiarity with the property due to lack of exposure. Children may not generalize their reasoning across properties, so they need to discover the reasoning through experience with each property. It is important to note that some researchers do not feel the concept of

stages is useful because it conceals the fact that each stage involves gradual transitions which occur over long periods of time and which vary widely depending on individual ability.

The Concept of Number. Preschoolers are usually able to count from one to ten. However, their understanding of the concept of number is quite limited. Thus, when counting objects, they do not necessarily recognize the importance of **one-to-one correspondence**, that each object should be counted once and only to know the sum of objects. In determining number, they are likely to respond to other features of the stimuli (e.g., size).

Classification. Beginning to understand concepts such as "more than" and "less than" as well as **class inclusion**, that there are subordinate and superordinate groups that are in a hierarchical relationship, enables school-aged children to understand and solve numerical problems. Understanding hierarchical structure also aids children's understanding of the social world, in terms of the multiple roles people play and of academic subjects such as geography (a continent contains countries which contain states, etc.).

Seriation refers to the ability to order objects in a logical progression (e.g., sticks in order by length). While a four-year-old can arrange two or three sticks in size order, it is not until approximately age 7 that children approach seriation tasks in a systematic manner. This suggests that by age 7, children are capable of **transitive reasoning**, which refers to the ability to recognize a relationship between two objects by knowing their relationship to a third.

Environmental Influences on Attainment of Concrete Operational Thought:

Although Piaget did all of his observations with middle-income children of culturally homogeneous Western backgrounds, subsequent research conducted in many cross-cultural settings confirms the fact that children around the world follow the same basic sequence of development; they proceed from the sensorimotor to the preoperational to the concrete operational period. However, the rate of progression differs within different cultures. For example, children exposed to clay through pottery-making will develop conservation of mass earlier than children who do not experience clay daily.

Several cross-cultural studies found that in some cultures children ages 12 or 13 as well as some adults do not evidence an understanding of conservation. These studies have been criticized because the experimenters failed to consider the impact of the language used in the testing situation.

The Role of Training. Studies have also been conducted to determine whether or not children's acquisition of concrete operations can be accelerated through training. These studies demonstrate that it is possible to accelerate children's acquisition to some extent. However, some researchers have challenged whether or not hurrying cognitive development is good educational practice. While children outgrow the reasoning of the preschool period, this form of reasoning may be useful in later life in the process of imagination and creativity.

Piaget and Education:

Piaget did not believe in training and saw attempts to train children as succeeding only in modifying verbal responses. Piaget argued that children must be allowed opportunities to learn through self-initiated interaction with the physical environment in order to discover solutions. "Each time someone prematurely teaches a child something he could discover for himself, that child is kept from inventing it and consequently from understanding it completely" (Piaget, 1970). **Open classrooms**, which provide children with less structured settings in which exploration is encouraged, developed in part in response to Piaget's theory.

LANGUAGE DEVELOPMENT

Metalinguistic Awareness:

Metalinguistic awareness refers to children's intuitive understanding of how language works (e.g., knowing whether a sentence is correct and whether an ambiguous sentence has two meanings. It emerges at approximately age 5 and continues to develop throughout middle childhood. This is not to be confused with the ability to talk about language, which is called **metalanguage** (e.g., verbs, nouns, clauses). It may not be surprising that metalinguistic awareness develops most rapidly during the elementary school years. Indeed, some researchers have contended that the development of metalinguistic awareness is closely related to academic experiences. Metalinguistic awareness is evident in two basic changes during the middle childhood years: communicative competence and understanding metaphors.

Communicative Competence. When a preschool child is asked whether a sentence is correct, the child cannot differentiate between the **meaning** or content of the sentence and the **structure**.

While most simple grammatical rules are mastered during the preschool years, the ability to access and use explicit knowledge about **syntax**, the underlying grammatical rules specifying the order and function of words in a sentence, develops throughout the middle school years. In addition, school-aged children can think about whether instructions are adequate and have a greater capacity to understand complex grammatical sentences. School-aged children also develop much more precise meanings for words.

Understanding Metaphors. Language during the middle childhood years becomes increasingly nonliteral, which enables them to understand and appreciate metaphors. While children who are 7 and 8 understand that words such as sweet and bright can refer to both food and people, not until approximately age 10 or 11 are they able to understand figures of speech and explain the relation between the literal and nonliteral meanings of words. This is accompanied by the ability to think of psychological traits in nonliteral as well as literal terms (e.g., understanding how a hard rock might bear a resemblance to a person being stubborn).

Interpreting metaphors involves two cognitive processes: 1) understanding figurative language; and 2) creating a meaning for the metaphor similar to that of adults. Five-year-old children are able to accomplish the first task. However, they appear to have difficulty with the second task.

145

Humor:

   During the school-age years children begin to
appreciate riddles which rely on words having double
meanings and they love to engage in play on words (puns)
and jokes involving double meanings. These jokes often
rely on decentering, holding two features of the word in
mind, reversibility, shifting attention between the two
meanings, as well as reclassification of a word according
to another context (e.g., What has an ear but cannot
hear? -- corn). Humor is appreciated when it offers a
moderate amount of intellectual challenge. Thus, jokes
deemed too simple for adults are hysterically funny to
middle school-aged children.

Language-Minority Children:

   For many children language presents a barrier
rather than an opportunity for learning. **Language-
minority** children begin school unable to speak English.
There is controversy regarding whether it is best to
mainstream these children in English-speaking classes
(either with or without language help) or whether it is
better to place these children in classes conducted in
their native tongue. It is important to recognize that
there are many different language-minority children.

   <u>Bilingual children</u> are children who grow up hearing
and speaking two languages. There is "bilingualism as a
first language," where children grow up speaking two
languages, and there is bilingualism through learning two
languages consecutively (second-language learners). Most
of the research which has been conducted has been on
second-language learners. When a child is raised in a
bilingual environment from infancy, he will learn two
separate grammatical systems and two separate
vocabularies. While initially both languages will be
mixed, by approximately age two, the child begins to
distinguish between two vocabularies and two grammatical
systems. With second-language learners there is often
mixing of languages. There is evidence that some of this
may not be confusion. Rather, the child is **code-
switching**, or deliberately borrowing a word or phrase
from the other language. While once viewed as a
detriment to cognitive development, there is now evidence
that bilingual children show enhanced metalinguistic
ability. However, bilingualism is not always associated

with a cognitive advantage. When both languages are valued by the culture children are more likely to evidence cognitive advantage. In contrast, bilingual children are likely to evidence difficulties when the home language is not valued by society, or when children decide to replace the home language with the dominant language prior to their parents' learning to speak the dominant language. In the latter instance, since adults learn languages more slowly than children, parents may not be able to provide an enriched language environment in the dominant language because they are not yet facile with metaphoric language.

   Bilingual Education. The majority of bilingual children in America are second-language learners who are in a situation of subtractive bilingualism because society does not value their home language or the fact that they are bilingual. Thus, they are under pressure to replace their home language with English. Bilingual programs focusing on native-language instruction typically involve teaching children content matter in their native tongue for approximately half of the day and providing youngsters with intensive English language training for the remainder of the day. Advocates of this method argue that teaching children skills such as literacy in their native language provides a strong cognitive foundation that will serve general academic development as well as the acquisition of a second language.

   Nonstandard English. Some black children from low-income families share many problems faced by bilingual children. While their native language is English, they speak a nonstandard dialect, or Black English, which is different not only in its intonation patterns and vocabulary but in its grammar and pronunciation. Initially thought to be the result of language deprivation, it is now recognized that Black English is governed by its own set of grammatical rules. Since standard English is the primary means of communication and instruction in schools, black children using Black English are at a disadvantage until they acquire proficiency in standard English.

THE CHILD IN SCHOOL

The School as a Learning Environment:

Throughout the middle school years children spend a great deal of their time in school or performing school-related tasks. Thus, school influences a child's values, self-esteem, achievement orientation, and learning. Increasingly during this period children learn concepts in school which are set apart from concrete referents or contexts. In addition, children must follow specific instructions and engage in predominantly unidirectional conversations in which they are listeners who are periodically asked to respond in a highly structured manner. This is quite a different experience from the apprenticeships, or on-the-job training involving observation and interaction that occurs in other cultures.

In our own complex society, schooling is not only universally available but also compulsory. In most countries, formal schooling does not begin until the child is between 5 and 7. This is because after the five-to-seven shift children are better able to follow instructions, apply reasoning and memory skills to problem solving, concentrate on learning specific tasks, and learn and operate according to rules.

Learning from Other Cultures: The Effects of Schooling on Cognitive Development:

While there are limitations to cross-cultural studies of the relation between schooling and cognitive development, the results have shown that children attending school do better on some cognitive tasks involving memory and classification. Researchers have also found that school experience enhances language development and increases children's lexicons, or the total number of words in their vocabulary.

Learning Problems:

American school children's achievement levels are lower today than they were 20 years ago and are lower than those of their peers in other developed countries (e.g., Japan, China). These findings raise significant concern because children who fail in school will be at great risk in negotiating adult life. In addition, a well-educated work force is central to maintaining a leadership role among advanced technological societies and competing economically in the world market.

Recommended reforms to improve American education include: raising teacher salaries, mandating competency testing for teachers, increasing the number of required math and science courses, and increasing the amount of time children actually spend at school. Changes in family structure may also reduce the amount of time parents are available to engage in educational activities with their children (e.g., reading, helping with homework).

Motivation for Learning. **Competence motivation** refers to children's intrinsic motivation to learn and understand the world around them. To the extent that curiosity and independent exploration are rewarded, either through praise, approval, or the experience of success, motivation will increase. However, when punished or ignored, children learn to rely on adults and avoid learning situations. Indifference to children's efforts may lead some children to give up on the task at hand and after repeated failures to believe that they cannot succeed. Children with an attributional style of **learned helplessness** believe that their effort will not lead to success and that they have no control over whether they do well or poorly. They tend to attribute the outcome of school tasks to external events (e.g., luck, a good or bad teacher). It is important to note that competence motivation varies with the task being learned. A child may feel very competent about reading but avoid mathematics.

Family Influences. Parental values and behavior influence children's competence motivation. Parents who are more involved in academic and related activities with their children, have higher expectations for their children, and provide support and encouragement are more likely to have children who succeed in school. They also tend to be parents who are more educated themselves.

Parental Involvement. The policy implications of these findings indicate that educators need to instill in parents the awareness that they are partners in their children's education and therefore must participate in school activities. Efforts to bring parents and schools together intensified when educators recognized that parent participation was a significant factor in the success of early intervention programs such as Project Head Start. Indeed, the federal government has mandated that any federally funded program serving young children must include a parent-involvement component. Other parental involvement programs (e.g., Follow Through) have demonstrated that parental involvement increases academic achievement.

Anxiety. Children may fail to learn because they are too anxious or emotionally upset to pay attention to what is going on in the classroom. These emotional difficulties may result from family stresses at home (e.g., divorce, family violence, poverty), difficulties learning in school, or a severe emotional disorder in the child.

Learning Disabilities. Learning disabled children typically have average or above average intelligence but are delayed in their performance on academic tasks such as mathematics or reading. Their difficulties are not a result of emotional difficulties, lack of motivation, or stress at home. However, when children are having significant difficulties learning and they do not receive adequate supports in the school, emotional and behavioral difficulties may develop. **Dyslexia** is a term used to describe many different kinds of learning disabilities which result in impaired reading. Some emotional and behavioral difficulties may be more directly related to the underlying cognitive difficulties causing the learning disability. For example, the child whose reading disability is related to a larger language processing deficit may also have difficulty following verbal instructions. Other children may have difficulty decoding nonverbal cues and therefore have difficulty in social situations.

There is increasing evidence that some learning disabilities are inherited. Also, researchers are becoming aware that children do not outgrow learning disabilities. Rather, they can learn to compensate for the disability.

Discussion of Social Issues: Mainstreaming:

   The Education of All Handicapped Children Act
(Public Law 94-142) guarantees every handicapped child an
appropriate public education individually tailored to
meet his or her specific needs and the least restrictive
placement that is appropriate. Thus, many children who
in the past were placed in separate classrooms for
handicapped children are currently being **mainstreamed,** or
placed with non-handicapped youngsters. Another
important component of the legislation is its mandate for
parents' participation in developing individualized
instruction for their children.

   Although the intent of PL94-142 is to destigmatize
handicapped children, some researchers have vigorously
debated its wisdom. A child with special needs requires
not only the opportunity to socialize with non-
handicapped youngsters but also opportunities to learn
specialized skills (e.g., a hearing-impaired child may
need to learn sign language). Mainstream teachers may
not have adequate training to provide for the special
needs of handicapped youngsters. In addition, some
researchers have found that mainstreamed children may
have lower self-esteem than children who are in
classrooms for handicapped children. Due to these
controversies and to variability in the funding levels in
different school districts, there is considerable
variability in the manner in which PL94-142 has been
implemented.

   This variability in implementation points to the
need to evaluate any social policy which is endorsed
through legislation. First, we need to conduct **process
evaluation**, to verify that the services mandated by the
policy are in fact delivered. Second, **outcome
evaluation**, which assesses the impact of the policy and
addresses whether the services mandated are resulting in
positive effects for children, must be conducted. Both
types of evaluation yield important lessons so that any
discrepancies between the policy's initial intent and
its outcome can be minimized.

KEY TERMS AND CONCEPTS

Fill in the blank with the word or phrase that best completes the sentence. Check your answers against the Answer Key.

1. Images are retained for less than a second in _____ memory.

2. _____, and not just IQ, should be considered when defining mental retardation.

3. Tying a string around your finger to help you remember something is a strategy employed only by those who have acquired _____.

4. The inability to speak or comprehend spoken language is called _____.

5. A child who arranges a set of sticks in ascending order of length is demonstrating _____.

6. Metalinguistic awareness appears at about age _____.

7. Language skills related to everyday informal communication are called _____ language skills.

8. _____ refers to the child's ability to focus on relevant aspects of a situation.

9. Middle childhood corresponds with the Piagetian _____ stage.

10. The child's ability to draw conclusions based on prior relationships is called _____.

MULTIPLE CHOICE SELF-TEST

_____1. During the Middle Ages, the 7-year-old was
  a. expected to be seen and not heard
  b. considered ready to take on adult roles
  c. still confined to the nursery
  d. kept with his mother at all times

_____2. According to information processing theory, the
       school-aged child is ready to benefit from
       formal schooling because
  a. of her preschool and kindergarten training
  b. she is big enough to sit still for six hours
  c. of her large vocabulary
  d. of her increased capacity to process
       information

_____3. Selective attention refers to
  a. the child's ability to focus on relevant
       aspects of a situation
  b. the child's ability to select tasks which are
       appropriate for her attention
  c. the child who only pays attention when he wants
       to
  d. educational policies that track children
       according to their attention spans

_____4. In _____ memory, impressions are
       retained only for a second, then transferred to
       the next level of information storage.
  a. short-term
  b. sensory
  c. recognition
  d. long-term

_____5. Which item is not a memory-aiding device?
  a. mnemonic strategies
  b. external aids
  c. rehearsal
  d. metamemory

_____6. Middle childhood corresponds to the Piagetian
_____ stage.
   a. concrete operational
   b. preoperational
   c. latency
   d. formal operational

_____7. Piaget's concrete operational stage includes
        children from about
   a. birth to 2 or 3
   b. adolescence to adulthood
   c. preschool to school age
   d. 7-12

_____8. Which of these is irrelevant to children's
        performance on tests of conservation?
   a. inability to distinguish between "same" and
      "different"
   b. the language used in the test
   c. familiarity with the material used
   d. children's age

_____9. Verbal humor is most appreciated when it
   a. offers some intellectual challenge
   b. can be "gotten" with no mental effort
   c. is equally accessible to children and adults
   d. is funny to children but not adults

_____10. Children who are bilingual from infancy
   a. usually perform poorly in both languages
   b. never fully cease to confuse the two languages
   c. often display precocious metalinguistic skills
   d. score well in one language and poorly in the
      other

RECOMMENDATIONS FOR FURTHER READING

Adams, M. J. (1990). Beginning to Read: Thinking and Learning about Print. Cambridge, MA: The MIT Press.

Kail, R. (1990). The Development of Memory in Children. New York: W. H. Freeman Press.

National Association for the Education of Young Children (1988). Position statement on standardized testing of young children 3 through 8 years of age. Young Children, March.

Perlmutter, M. (1980). Children's Memory. New Directions for Child Development, No. 10. San Fransisco: Jossey-Bass.

Wellman, H. M. (1990). The Child's Theory of Mind. Cambridge, MA: MIT Press.

ANSWER KEY FOR SELF-TEST ITEMS

Key Terms and Concepts

1. sensory
2. social competence
3. metamemory
4. aphasia
5. seriation
6. 5
7. contextualized
8. selective attention
9. concrete operational
10. reversibility

Multiple Choice

1.	b	6.	a
2.	d	7.	d
3.	a	8.	a
4.	b	9.	a
5.	d	10.	c

CHAPTER 13

SOCIAL AND EMOTIONAL DEVELOPMENT
DURING MIDDLE CHILDHOOD

STUDY GOALS

While studying Chapter 13, you should focus on:

1. The school-age child's sense of self, and influences on self-esteem.

2. Middle childhood's advances in perspective-taking and social interactions involving acquaintances and peers, teachers, and family members.

3. The child's social development in relation to the larger community, including moral development, social skills training, and the evolution of children's rules.

4. Social policy issues related to the social and emotional development of school-age children, including poverty, stress, and child care issues.

CHAPTER OVERVIEW

PROGRESS IN SOCIAL AND EMOTIONAL DEVELOPMENT

In the middle school years children become increasingly self-reliant. At the same time children expand their circle of friends and the world of peers becomes increasingly important.

Advances in Social Cognition. In the middle school years children make tremendous gains in their ability to think about social relationships. This includes the developing understanding of others' feelings and intentions and children's recognition that other people think about the intentions and feelings they may experience. **Role-taking**, or **perspective-taking**, which refers to the child's comprehension of information about another person's internal experiences, enables children to make inferences about others' psychological experiences and states.

Selman (1976, 1980) identified four levels of role-taking between the ages of 4 and 12 years:

Level 0, Egocentric Role-Taking -- not yet distinguishing between their own perspective and that of others, children assume that others have feelings and thoughts more or less identical to their own;

Level 1, Subjective Role-Taking -- by approximately age 4, children begin to realize that others think or feel differently because they are in a different situation or know different information. They also realize two people may interpret the same event differently. However, it is difficult to hold both perspectives simultaneously;

Level 2, Self-Reflective Role-Taking -- by approximately age 6, children are aware that people think or feel differently because different people have different values and recognize that there may be more than one correct position in a given situation. They can now think about how others view them and anticipate how others will react to their own actions and ideas.

Level 3, Mutual Role-Taking -- by approximately age 10, children are able not only to differentiate their own perspective from that of other people, they can also think about their own point of view and that of the other person simultaneously.

Level 4, Societal or In-Depth Perspective -- this last stage, which emerges between age 12 and adulthood, is characterized by the ability to take a generalized perspective of society and its laws, which involves the realization that people do not always understand others' values.

Other researchers argue against such a stage theory and state that when play is examined, in contrast to discussing situations with children, role-taking can be observed in preschool children. Also, they point out that a child who is skilled at taking the perspective of familiar people in familiar situations may have more difficulty generalizing to unfamiliar people in unfamiliar settings. Finally, researchers point out that social experience (e.g., peer interaction) facilitates social role-taking skills. In turn, children who have

good social role-taking skills are better at initiating
and maintaining friendships. This is because effective
communication depends on evaluating what others already
know and anticipating what they need to know or are
interested in knowing.

 Moral Development. Progress in social cognition
also enhances children's ability to evaluate their own
behavior in relation to what others think and feel and in
relation to socially acceptable patterns of behavior.
Each society has explicit and implicit rules about
people's moral behavior. One's **conscience** reflects the
internalization of standards of right and wrong in our
family, community, and society.

 The Development of Moral Knowledge. In an effort to
understand how children learn the difference between
right and wrong psychoanalysts focus on the emotional
aspects of moral development such as guilt and anxiety
and the resolution of the Oedipal conflict. In contrast,
social learning theorists contend that we learn social
norms through modeling and reinforcement. Cognitive-
developmental theorists do not believe that morality
develops as a result of external influences. Instead,
they believe that we develop our moral reasoning
progressively along with our cognitive abilities. For
example, Piaget was interested in how children thought
about and followed rules in a game. In this manner he
gained insights about moral development in terms of
issues such as fairness, reciprocity, and justice. It is
only in the middle school years that children begin to
play by the rules.

 Preschoolers view rules as absolute and unchangeable
but in games will change the rules to suit themselves.
In contrast, school-aged children are very strict about
following the rules in a game and consider it cheating to
arbitrarily change the rules in the course of a game. By
the end of the middle school years, children recognize
that rules are not absolute. Instead, they reason that
since the purpose of the rules is to benefit all who are
involved, the participants can change and reformulate the
rules through reasoning, discussions, and general
agreement. Similarly, children aged 5 to 10 may judge
the seriousness of a transgression by its consequences
irrespective of the intent of the actor. However, by age
11, most children will judge the seriousness of a

transgression on the basis of the intention of the actor (purposive vs. accidental).

Kohlberg's Stages of Moral Development. Building upon Piaget, Kohlberg proposed six (later revised to five) stages of moral development grouped within three levels of moral thought:

The Preconventional Level -- children's emphasis is on avoiding punishment and getting a reward.

Stage 1 -- children value **obedience to authority.** Decisions are based on concrete consequences (e.g., follow rules to avoid punishment).
Stage 2 -- the **instrumental relativist stage.** Children take care of their own needs (e.g., be nice to others so they will be nice to you).

The Conventional Level -- Emphasis is on social rules and on maintaining the expectations of the individual's family, group, or society.

Stage 3 -- the **good-girl and nice-boy orientation** stage. A behavior is right if it meets with other people's approval.
Stage 4 -- the **law-and-order orientation.** A behavior is right if it consists of doing one's duty and showing respect for authority.

The Postconventional or Autonomous Level -- There is a clear effort on the part of the individual to define moral values and principles that have validity and application.

Stage 5 -- the **social contract or legalistic orientation.** The individual recognizes that laws serve the common good. Right actions are defined in terms of the balance between individual rights and standards set by society.
Stage 6 -- **universal ethical principles orientation.** The individual acquires a personal commitment to moral principles because of the rational recognition of universal concepts. The role of personal ethics in defining what is right is acknowledged. This stage was later merged with stage 5.

Kohlberg's theory has had extensive influence on

educators. One procedure labeled **value clarification** involves encouraging children to think about their values through discussions of hypothetical dilemmas.

Some researchers have criticized Kohlberg's use of dilemmas which involve rule breaking. For example, using stories that depict everyday examples, Damon notes four domains of moral development: positive justice (fairness), friendships, obedience to authority, and social rules and conventions. Others have criticized Kohlberg for failing to look at sex differences in children's answers to moral dilemmas and for basing his studies on males' responses. For example, Gilligan (1982) argues Kohlberg's stages are not appropriate to women because women are more concerned with relationships and social responsibilities and use them in moral reasoning whereas men are more concerned with legal issues and rules.

Moral Behavior. Researchers have also observed that children and adults often do not behave in a manner which is consistent with the moral standards they endorse verbally. Behavioral controls range from external to internal and include factors such as social approval (e.g., parents) and punishment. Hoffman distinguishes two disciplinary strategies parents adopt: 1) Punitive techniques emphasize the personal consequences of breaking rules; 2) Inductive methods emphasize the effects of misbehavior on the victims of moral transgressions.

Advances in the Self-Concept. During the middle school years children acquire a more refined sense of their gender identities and gender roles and continue the process of differentiating themselves from others in their surroundings. They develop a picture of a unique, complex, and multifaceted self. Increasingly they are aware of their inner thoughts and feelings and recognize that they are changing.

How Do I Feel about Myself? In addition to developing a more complex self-view, children in the middle school years begin to judge how worthy they are. This **evaluative component of the self-concept** is important to mental health and peer relations in middle childhood and later life. Erik Erikson stressed the importance of the development of self-esteem during this period, noting that the child then undergoes the psychological crisis of **industry vs. inferiority**. He theorized that the child who can find and concentrate on areas of strength and success gains a sense of mastery, or industry. In contrast, a child who cannot find areas of competency soon develops a sense of inferiority and feels insignificant in comparison with others.

Influences on Self-Esteem:

Family Influences. Interactions with parents largely determine the child's sense of self-esteem. When parents consider the child's opinion and allow him to express himself they convey that they think the child is an important and worthy individual. Further, when parents set clear and realistic limits for children and are consistent the child is more likely to meet parental expectations for behavior. When rules are ambiguous, children have more difficulty monitoring, evaluating, and regulating their own behavior.

After the child enters school peers and teachers play an increasingly powerful role as socialization agents. Sometimes, children face conflicting messages about behavior between school and home.

THE SOCIAL WORLD OF THE SCHOOL-AGE CHILD

The School:

Norms for behavior in school come from academic curriculum, which includes the tasks the child is expected to master, and from the hidden curriculum, which refers to the mechanisms maintaining order and control in the classroom. School success will depend in part on how quickly the student can learn and adjust to the assigned student and teacher roles (e.g., obeying instructions, being quiet in class).

The Influence of Teachers. Teachers' attitudes toward the children in their classes often play a large role in how the child feels about being at school and about himself. **Teacher expectations**, or beliefs about students' competencies, strongly influence student learning. Randomly assigning children to high or low teacher expectations resulted in raised and lowered IQ scores respectively. Some pupils may begin to act in ways that are consistent with the teacher's expectations, setting in motion a self-fulfilling prophecy. This sequence is especially likely to occur in the first and second grades of school, when children are still forming an initial impression of school norms and standards for behavior. Teacher expectations of children's performance can be conveyed nonverbally (e.g., more smiling, eye contact, head nods) and expectations are not typically related to children's actual abilities. Expectations are often based on racial and gender stereotypes, child attractiveness, or even on the attractiveness of children's names.

A Society of Children:

During middle childhood children are spending increasing amounts of time with their peers. They become a part of what social scientists refer to as a **society of children**, that has its own rituals, traditions, activities, and rules as well as its own songs and games. Increasingly, adults are excluded from these peer interactions.

Forming Groups. Groups which form at this age are characterized by common goals, aims, and rules of social conduct. At ages 6-7, peer groups are play groups, but by age 9, a hierarchical structure that identifies each member's relationship to others in the group is apparent. Typically, one member is a leader. By the end of this period, peer groups are generally informal cliques of two-three members, who play important roles in the child's development. Also at this time, children may begin to evidence an interest in members of the opposite sex and may spend a great deal of time discussing concerns related to growing up.

Close Friends. By age 10-11, children may experience very intense friendships in which they share their innermost thoughts and feelings and can provide emotional support. Children also view trust as a basic tenet of a friendship.

Peer Acceptance. Children tend to include other children who are perceived to be sociable, funny, and similar to themselves; they tend to exclude children who seem odd or different in appearance, skills, or temperament.

Popular Children. Using a technique called **sociometry**, researchers ask children within an organized setting (e.g., classroom) to name the child or children who fit categories such as "best friend," "best liked," or "most aggressive." Based on the children's answers they draw a **sociogram**, a graphic representation of how each child in the group is perceived by the others. Although no one quality makes a child popular, popular children are more likely to be outgoing, sensitive and accepting of others, and cooperative. Popularity is also related to IQ and academic achievement. Moderately achieving children are most likely to be popular.

In addition to popularity, ethnic background and sex often determine group membership. **Sex cleavage** is a term which reflects the tendency of boys and girls to choose to play with same sex age-mates.

Conformity. During the school-aged years children become increasingly likely to yield to peer pressure, conforming to the peer standards. This is due in part to the increasing desire to be accepted by members of the group. It is important to note that while style of dress may be readily influenced by peer standards, values and beliefs may continue to be influenced by parental standards.

The Family:

Changes in the Parent-Child Relationship. Parents spend approximately half as much time taking care of, reading to, and playing with their 5- to 12-year-old children as they do with children younger than five. In addition, new issues such as children's responsibilities for household chores and the kinds of friends they are spending time with emerge. This reflects the increasing role the child is playing in regulating his or her own behavior. Maccoby (1984) refers to this shared responsibility as **co-regulation**, noting that parents exert general supervisory control while children exercise moment to moment self-control. Parents continue to be important influences on children's self-esteem and academic development.

Realities of Family Life. In a large proportion of families both mother and father work. Some researchers report that there are increased strains associated with having to meet the obligations of job and family. Some husbands and wives have little time for socializing and for relaxed and entertaining family activities. The stress appears to be higher for women in dual career families, because they continue to bear primary responsibility for household work, childcare, and caring for elderly family members.

    <u>The Effects on Children</u>. In studying the effects of dual working families the age and sex of the child, the nature of the employment (full vs. part time, satisfying vs. non-satisfying) and the S.E.S. of the family must be taken into consideration. A national survey of school-aged children found that children complained their parents did not spend enough time with them. Similarly, surveys of mothers find that they wish they had more time with their children. However, studies on school-age children whose mothers are working reveal that maternal employment is generally associated with positive consequences for the children. Maternal employment contributes to girls' academic competence during the school years and later in life and to later occupational competence. While positive effects have generally been reported for girls, a study of boys in working-class families reported that the boys evidenced disturbed relationships with their fathers, were nervous, were disliked at school, and had low math and achievement scores.

Discussion of Social Issues: Children in Self-Care:

    <u>Latchkey Children</u>. Mother's satisfaction with employment is to some extent a function of the availability of adequate child care and on how the child fares while her parents are working. Unfortunately, due to a lack of adequate child care facilities for school-aged children, at least 2 to 4 million children between the ages of 6 and 13 stay home alone before and after school and during school vacations. At one time **children in self-care** were called **latchkey children** because they wore their keys on a string around their neck. The effects of being left alone vary according to the age of the child and the degree of structure and supervision provided children while they are alone (e.g., neighbors checking in). Low supervision is associated with increased drug and alcohol abuse. In some cases, children left alone become victims of sexual assaults and

other crimes. Many feel isolated, afraid, and lonely.

  <u>School-Age Child Care</u>. Many schools have set up
before- and after-school care which is paid for by parents
with the schools providing the space. Other solutions to
this problem involve more comprehensive efforts such as
the School for the 21st Century which provides school-age
care along with other family support services.

  <u>Single-Parent Families</u>. The need for after-school
care is especially acute for single-parent families in
which the only parent is working. Currently, one in four
children lives in a single-parent family (among blacks it
is one child in every two). While single-parent
families differ widely, 90 percent are headed by women
and most are the outcome of divorce. School-aged
children are better able to cope with divorce than
younger children. Being older they are better able to
understand that they are not to blame for the family
breakup. They are also more aware of their feelings and
better able to talk about them (e.g., sadness, anger).
Nevertheless, they often evidence behavioral and academic
difficulties at school. When parents maintain a good
relationship and fathers remain involved, the negative
effects of the divorce tend to diminish. Poverty is
another characteristic of many single-parent families.
In the United States, we have many more poor children
today than we did in the 1960s and poverty among
children is still increasing.

  Changes in federal assistance programs for the poor
have reduced the numbers of families who are eligible to
receive food stamps and other government assistance.
Poor children are most likely to reside in single-parent
families. Further, over one-third of Hispanic and close
to one-half of black children are currently living in
poverty. The effects of poverty on children are
widespread and include malnutrition, assaults on self-
esteem, increased mental health problems, and increased
failure in school. In addition, they are more likely to
feel that they cannot control their environment or future
and attribute success and failure to external factors.
The negative effects of poverty on children will vary
with its depth and duration and the parents' physical and
mental health and the availability of social supports.

Helping Children Cope with Stress:

Many children are unable to cope with their difficulties. Severe marital discord, low social status, overcrowding or large family size, and maternal psychiatric disorders are associated with behavioral and psychiatric disorders in children. Experiencing two or more of these risks simultaneously greatly increases children's risk for psychiatric disorders. At the same time, the influence of one close caring adult can serve as a buffer, protecting children who are at risk from the negative consequences of stressors. Thus, just as support services can help facilitate the lives of many parents, such services can also help children cope with the difficult realities of contemporary life.

KEY TERMS AND CONCEPTS

Complete these sentences, then check your responses against the Answer Key at the end of this chapter.

1.   The Eriksonian crisis to be resolved during middle childhood is _____.

2.   The _____ refers to the unspoken rules implicitly governing teacher-student interaction in the classroom.

3.   _____ of all U.S. children live in single-parent families.

4.   The preconventional, conventional, and postconventional are the major stages of moral development in _____'s theoretical formulation.
5.   Gilligan's work on moral development explores _____ in moral reasoning.

6.   Piaget and Inhelder's "3 mountains" paradigm was designed to examine children's _____ skills.

7.   After about age 11, children judge an act on _____.

8.   7- to 12-year-olds and especially 12-year-olds are especially susceptible to peer pressure because they place a high value on _____.

9. Children who care for themselves alone after school are called _____ children.

10. _____ refers to the child's ability to comprehend another person's perspective.

MATCHING

1. Piaget & Inhelder   a. industry v. inferiority

2. Selman   b. observational learning of moral development

3. Kohlberg   c. contemporary view of perspective-taking

4. Gilligan   d. resilience

5. Rosenthal & Jacobson   e. 3 mountains paradigm

6. Erikson   f. stages of moral development

7. Aronfreed   g. teacher's expectations

8. Rutter & Garmezy   h. sex differences in moral thought

_____1.   8-year-olds base judgments of blame on
   a.   the consequences of behavior
   b.   the intentions behind the behavior
   c.   whether they had ever been involved in a
        similar situation
   d.   the gender of the perpetrator

_____2.   Carol Gilligan's criticisms of Kohlberg's work
          are based on her perception of his
   a.   failure to remain methodologically rigorous
   b.   failure to include black subjects
   c.   failure to consider sex differences
   d.   overreliance on anecdotal evidence

_____3.   Rosenthal and Jacobson are known for their
          research on
   a.   ethnic differences in moral thought
   b.   parenting styles
   c.   the effect of teachers' expectations
   d.   peer acceptance among school children

_____4.   By the mid-1980s, there were roughly
          _____ latchkey children in the U.S.
   a.   50,000-60,000
   b.   2-4 million
   c.   500,000
   d.   14 million

_____5.   _____% of black children in the U.S. live in
          single-parent homes.
   a.   12
   b.   2
   c.   90
   d.   50

_____6.   Piaget's understanding of the development of
          children's rules was derived from his
          observations of
   a.   games of marbles
   b.   games of soccer
   c.   student governments
   d.   boy-girl interactions

_____7. Freud felt that the child's ability to later
            achieve psychosexual maturity was based on a
            resolution of
        a. the riddle of the Sphinx
        b. the Oedipal conflict
        c. narcissism
        d. the pleasure principle

_____8. The resilience of some children in the face of
            severe stressors is the focus of the research
            by
        a. Gilligan
        b. Rosenthal and Jacobson
        c. Piaget and Inhelder
        d. Rutter and Garmezy

_____9. 10- to 12-year-old boys typically respond to
            Kohlberg's Heinz story by saying
        a. his wife's life is more important than societal
            prohibitions against theft
        b. stealing violates absolute principles of social
            order
        c. Heinz's wife would die anyway, so theft is
            pointless
        d. Heinz would be more use to his wife if not in
            jail for theft

_____10. The typical latchkey child's greatest complaint
            involves
        a. not getting help with her homework
        b. being afraid
        c. being lonesome
        d. boredom

RECOMMENDATIONS FOR FURTHER READING

Dodge, K., Coie, J. D., Pettit, G. S., & Price, J. M. (1990). Peer status and aggression in boys' groups: Developmental and contextual analysis. Child Development, 61, 1289-1309.

Gilligan, C., et al. (Eds.). Mapping the Moral Domain. Cambridge, MA: Harvard University Press.

Kidder, T. (1989). Among Schoolchildren. Boston: Houghton Mifflin Co.

Kunkel, D., & Murray, J. (1991). Television, children and social policy: Issues and resources for child advocates. Journal of Clinical Child Psychology, 20, 88-93.

Opie, I. A., & Opie, P. (1987). The Lore and Language of Schoolchildren. New York: Oxford University Press.

Piaget, J. (1965). The Moral Judgment of the Child. New York: Free Press.

Postman, N. (1982). The Disappearance of Childhood. New York: Delacorte Press.

Rizzo, T. A. (1989). Friendship Development Among Children in School. Norwood, NJ: Ablex Publishing Corporation.

Sherif, M. (1988). The Robbers Cave Experiment: Intergroup Conflict and Cooperation. Middletown, CT: Wesleyan University Press.

Selman, R. L., & Schultz, L. H. (1990). Making a Friend in Youth: Developmental Theory and Pair Therapy. Chicago: University of Chicago Press.

Walker, L., & Taylor, J. H. (1991). Stage transition in moral reasoning: A longitudinal study of developmental processes. Developmental Psychology, 27, 330-337.

ANSWER KEY FOR SELF-TEST ITEMS

Key Terms and Concepts

1. industry vs. inferiority
2. hidden curriculum
3. half
4. Kohlberg
5. sex differences
6. perspective-taking
7. intentionality
8. conformity
9. latchkey children
10. role-taking

Matching

1-e; 2-c; 3-f; 4-h; 5-g; 6-a; 7-b; 8-d

Multiple Choice

1.	a	6.	a
2.	c	7.	b
3.	c	8.	d
4.	b	9.	b
5.	d	10.	b

CHAPTER 14

PHYSICAL DEVELOPMENT DURING ADOLESCENCE

STUDY GOALS

A thorough study of Chapter 14 should help you to understand the basic facts and concepts behind:

1. Physical aspects of adolescent development, including the onset of adolescence in both males and females, physical growth characteristic of this period, and the emergence of secondary sexual characteristics. How the end of adolescence is defined.

2. The interaction between behavioral, physiological, and cultural factors during this period. The major points of theories regarding whether or not adolescence is necessarily stressful and difficult.

3. The timing of sexual maturity, its implications for behavior and for personality development. Adolescent pregnancy and parenting, its impact on teen mothers, fathers, and their offspring.

4. Developmental psychopathology of adolescence, including eating disorders, depression, and teen suicide.

CHAPTER OVERVIEW

What Is Adolescence?

Puberty, the physiological event culminating in sexual maturity, is a process involving major and rapid bodily changes. Adolescents become taller, change in their body proportions, and experience sexual differentiation as they become capable of reproduction. Accompanying these physical changes are cognitive and social-emotional changes. Researchers disagree about whether or not adolescence is inherently stressful; researchers who believe adolescence is stressful do not agree about the cause(s) of the stress.

Adolescence as a Cultural Invention. It is only in
recent history that society has marked the period of
adolescence as a separate phase of development. Prior to
the late 18th century adolescents had full adult
responsibilities and privileges. The concept of
adolescence has been linked with specific changes in
societal conditions:

1. Increasingly specialized skills in the workplace
that required a longer course of formal education;
2. Three major social movements: compulsory
education, child labor legislation, and special
legal procedures developed for youth;
3. Adolescence is increasing in duration, in part
because children reach puberty at younger ages; and
4. Continued lengthening of formal education has
increased the length of adolescents' dependence on
their parents.

At this point in time it is very difficult to
specify when adolescence ends. Some define the end
chronologically, (e.g., age 18) while others specify its
ending when the individual assumes adult roles and
responsibilities (e.g., working, living independently).

The Passage to Adulthood. In some societies the
child becomes an adult at a certain age, and this passage
is marked by **puberty rites**, or ceremonies declaring the
individual's assumption of new adult roles in the
community. These ceremonies serve an important
psychological function for the individual, by providing
him or her with expectations and guidelines for meeting
societal standards. In our society, the period of
adolescence is not only longer, but there is no clear
boundary or point at which an individual is clearly
regarded as an adult. Thus, there are significant
variations in the ages at which an individual may drive a
car, marry, drink alcohol, vote, or own property.

Storm and Stress or Cultural Expectations. Many
social observers have characterized adolescence as a time
of deviation, rebellion, and emotional turmoil. However,
this view of adolescence is now changing. While some
individuals experience adolescence as a very stressful
period, many others do not.

G. Stanley Hall (1904) first named the phenomenon of adolescence, seeing it as a period of life beyond childhood but before the adoption of adult responsibilities. He viewed the storm, or emotional turbulence, of adolescence as a function of the biological changes the individual undergoes at this time. Psychoanalytic notions of adolescence as a conflictual time supported this view. However, Margaret Mead, using anthropological evidence from her studies of adolescence in Samoa, challenged this view and suggested that the turbulence we witness is a function of our culture's failure to provide clear expectations. Another non-biological explanation was offered by Kurt Lewin, who viewed adolescents as part of a marginal or minority group in society. Bandura focused on the expectations society has of adolescents to be rebellious and erratic. Several recent national and international studies of adolescents reported that a majority of individuals do not expereince turmoil during this phase of development. They have a good self-image and are emotionally healthy. At the same time, the physical events of adolescence do have a significant impact on the psychological functioning of a minority of individuals. Therefore the question we must ask is what kind of physiological changes produce problems among some adolescents, and under what circumstances? Further, we must place this question in the context of the cognitive, social, and cultural aspects of adolescence.

Physical Changes During Adolescence:

Puberty. The physical changes of puberty can be grouped into two categories: those related to physical growth and those related to the development of sexual characteristics. Hormones, chemical agents secreted into the bloodstream by the **master gland** or pituitary gland, cause both of these changes. The **hypothalamus**, a region of the brain at the base of the skull, signals the pituitary gland to produce hormones which in turn stimulate other endocrine glands (e.g., adrenal glands, ovaries in females, and testes in males) to secrete sex hormones. These sex hormones trigger changes in body function and structure.

Androgens are the male sex hormones (e.g., testosterone). Estrogen is the female sex hormone. Both androgens and estrogen are present in males and females

174

from prenatal development. Indeed, high levels of sex hormones during the prenatal period cause sexual differentiation. At the end of the prenatal period the production of hormones is suppressed and does not resume until about age seven when hormone levels begin to rise. By age 10 to 12, hormone levels become very high and puberty begins.

The Growth Spurt. During puberty both boys and girls undergo a period of rapid physical growth called a growth spurt which involves an initial weight gain followed by a spurt in height and changes in body proportions and dimensions. Girls begin their growth spurt two years ahead of boys (11 versus 13 years). However, there are large individual differences in the age at which children begin their growth spurt.

Changes in Body Proportion. Most noticeable in the changes in body parts and proportions is the growth of the hands, feet, and legs. Because these may take place at slightly different times, some adolescents may feel awkward and clumsy. The facial features characteristic of childhood disappear as the low forehead becomes wider, the mouth widens, and the lips become fuller. There is an increase in muscle growth (accompanied by increased strength) and a decrease in fat. Males gain more muscle tissue in this period than girls. Other changes include the growth of the heart and the capacity of the lungs. Boys develop larger hearts and greater lung capacity relative to their size than do girls. These changes enable many adolescents to become highly skilled athletes. During adolescence, sex differences in physical growth become pronounced.

Increased Nutritional Needs. The increased rate of growth during puberty is coupled with a natural increase in appetite. The nutrient most commonly deficient in the adolescent's diet is iron, and among girls who have started menstruating, iron deficiency anemia is very common. Undernourishment among teens is a critical problem. Misinformation about food values and increased reliance on fast-food restaurants where foods are high in fat contribute to undernutrition in adolescence.

Eating Disorders. Particularly in girls, the desire to achieve a slender "model's figure" may develop into an eating disorder. At the extreme is **anorexia nervosa**,

175

which is characterized by self-induced starvation, bizarre attitudes toward food, and a distorted body image. These girls are preoccupied with food, exercise, and dieting and view themselves as fat even when they are literally dying from starvation. Media images of our cultural value on thinness, adolescent issues related to control, autonomy, fears of growing up and perfectionism, parental rejection, and depression have all been theoretically linked to anorexia. Another eating disorder of teenage girls and young women is **bulimia**, which is characterized by binge eating followed by self-induced vomiting and/or use of laxatives. Some individuals suffer from both anorexia nervosa and bulimia. Psychotherapy for girls and young women suffering from eating disorders is often effective (e.g., behavior therapy, family therapy).

Sexual Maturation. The increased level of hormones discussed above stimulates the growth of the uterus and the thickening of the vaginal lining in girls. In boys, the penis grows and thickens and about a year later the scrotal sac enlarges. The physiological event signaling fertility in girls is **menarche**, the first menstrual period. Boys reportedly achieve reproductive potential when **ejaculation**, the discharge of seminal fluid containing sperm, first occurs. However, these physiological changes do not always indicate reproductive capability but rather should be viewed as one of a series of events leading toward full sexual maturity.

Secondary Sex Characteristics. By the end of puberty, most boys have wide shoulders and relatively narrow, slim hips. Girls have wider, more rounded hips and narrow shoulders.

Breasts. In girls, the growth of the breast "bud," which occurs when a small concentration of fat causes a slight rise of the breast, is one of the first signs that puberty has begun. The breasts continue to develop gradually for the next several years. Breast changes also occur in boys. Their **areola**, the pigmented area around the nipple, grows slightly larger in diameter. Many boys experience what they consider to be abnormal breast enlargement, but this development is usually temporary and subsides within a year or two.

Hair Growth. For boys and girls, the hair on the head

and body becomes darker and coarser. Next, hair grows in regions of the body which were previously smooth: pubic, axillary (underarm), and for boys facial and chest hair.

Voice. The voices of boys and girls change during puberty, becoming lower as the larynx enlarges and the length of the vocal cords increases. Termed **breaking of the voice**, this change is more pronounced in boys.

Acne. Acne occurs when glands in the skin, stimulated by androgens, produce a fatty substance called **sebum**. Sebum can clog pores, causing black- or whiteheads and pimples.

Hormonal Effects on Behavior.

There is some indication that hormones affect emotions and behavior. For example, some researchers report changes in girls' moods in the days prior to menstruation. High androgen secretion is believed to affect sex drive. In animal studies, high levels of androgen secretions influence assertiveness, dominance, and the sex drive. Other animal studies demonstrate the reciprocal influence between hormones and behavior by documenting that social experiences influence hormone levels.

Sexual Activity among Adolescents.

The number of sexually active teens has increased dramatically since the mid-1960s, with more boys reporting being sexual active than girls. This may be part of our society's **double standard**, or different set of rules for female and male sexuality. Until recently, psychologists believed that the male sex drive was much stronger than the female sex drive and thus it was the males' destiny to be dominant and sexually aggressive.

Sexually Transmitted Diseases.

The trend toward increased teen sexual activity is of great concern due to the increase in teen pregnancy and the sexually transmitted diseases. Sexual activity among teens is the most significant risk factor for contracting AIDS. In addition to AIDS, sexually active teens are at risk for contracting other common sexually transmitted diseases such as **chlamydia**, tiny bacteria infecting the reproductive tract, and **herpes**, which causes sores and blisters in the genital area. Untreated, chlamydia in females can lead to infertility. Herpes, which is difficult to treat, appears to significantly increase risk for cervical cancer, and babies exposed to the virus during birth are at risk for brain damage.

PHYSICAL CHANGES OF ADOLESCENCE: IMPACT ON PSYCHOLOGICAL FUNCTIONING

The Timing of Puberty:

The age at which one reaches puberty is not medically significant but does appear to influence self-concept. For girls, maturing either early or late can be a source of great embarrassment and concern. Boys who mature early are more likely to evidence positive self-esteem while late-maturing boys are more likely to evidence negative self-esteem. Some studies find that these differences in feelings are likely to persist long after there are no differences in physical attractiveness or size. Others have not reported long-lasting effects.

Cultural Variations. The psychological impact of early and late maturing is largely determined by cultural factors.

Depression during Adolescence:

Early adolescence is associated with a marked rise in the incidence of depression. Stressors including arguments with parents in early adolescence, the search for self-identity and independence, and the formation of close social and sexual relationships outside the family all contribute to the increased risk for difficulties in self-esteem and depression.

Adolescent Suicide. Depressed adolescents often think of committing suicide. While adolescent suicide is not new, it has been increasing and is currently the third leading cause of death among adolescents, after accidents and homicide. These three account for three-quarters of adolescent deaths. For every successful suicide there are 50 to 100 attempts. In addition, many deaths which are attributed to accidents are actually due to suicide. **Suicide clusters**, in which one successful suicide triggers several other attempted or successful suicides by friends or community members, is a related phenomenon. Researchers have not yet explained sufficiently the dramatic increase in adolescent suicide. Media coverage may actually increase suicidal behavior. The following factors are associated with an increased risk for suicide: social disruptions resulting from frequent changes, experience with violence or suicide, a previous arrest, a previous hospitalization for psychiatric illness or substance abuse, or the loss of a girlfriend or a boyfriend during the preceding year. Suicide often comes as a surprise to family and friends but often there are warning signs. A drastic change in personal appearance or behavior, excessive guilt or shame, abuse of drugs or alcohol, or talking about death are possible warning signals.

KEY TERMS AND CONCEPTS

After completing each sentence with the best word or phrase, check your answers at the end of the chapter.

1. The first major text on adolescence as a stage of life was written by _____.

2. Ceremonies marking an individual's entry into young adulthood are known as _____.

3. The portion of the brain that signals the pituitary gland to produce hormones is the _____.

4. The _____ gland is known as the master gland.

5. _____ is the female sex hormone.

6. _____ are the male sex hormones.

7. _____ hormones are responsible for puberty's rapid growth spurt.

8. _____ felt that adolescents were treated like, and thus behaved like, members of a minority group.

9. _____ is Greek for "great hunger."

10. Breaking of the voice in male adolescents is caused by enlargement of the _____.

MATCHING EXERCISE

1. G. Stanley Hall   a. 1914 study of teen suicide

2. Margaret Mead   b. puberty rites

3. Albert Bandura   c. teen as "marginal man"

4. Kurt Lewin   d. adolescence in Samoa

5. Kikuyu   e. suicide prevention

6. Simmons and Blyth   f. first book on adolescence

7. Lewis Terman   g. cultural expectations

8. Tishler   h. early vs. late maturation

MULTIPLE CHOICE SELF-TEST

_____1. Before the 17th century, adolescence in America
a. was very much as it is today
b. was regarded as a special period for schooling
c. did not exist as such
d. was a difficult period for girls, but easy for boys

_____2. How does the length of adolescence today compare with its length 50 years ago?
a. it is longer today
b. it is shorter today
c. it is the same today as 50 years ago
d. no data are available

_____3. Adolescence was first described as a period of "storm and stress" by
a. Sigmund Freud
b. Kurt Lewin
c. Anna Freud
d. G. Stanley Hall

_____4. Kurt Lewin felt that the adolescent was treated
like
a. a miniature adult
b. a member of a minority group
c. an infant
d. a sacred cow

_____5. The male hormones as a group are called
a. hypothalamus
b. estrogens
c. testosterones
d. androgens

_____6. Hormones produced by the pituitary gland
stimulate
a. other endocrine glands
b. the hypothalamus
c. the master gland
d. no other glands

_____7. Sexual differentiation first occurs
a. at menarche or first ejaculation
b. at about 6 weeks after conception
c. during the 2nd trimester of pregnancy
d. shortly before birth

_____8. The adolescent growth spurt occurs
a. earlier in boys than girls
b. earlier in girls than boys
c. at about the same age in girls and boys
d. with such variation that no rule can be stated

_____9. Death rates from starvation among anorexic
girls are
a. negligible, no one really dies from it
b. about 35%
c. virtually 100%
d. 5-15%

_____10. In bulimia, affected individuals
a. eat compulsively at all times
b. go through cycles of eating binges and purges
c. starve themselves to model thinness
d. are always clinically obese

RECOMMENDATIONS FOR FURTHER READING

Adams, G. R., Montemayor, R., & Gullotta, T. P. (1989). Biology of Adolescent Development and Behavior. Newbury Park, CA: Sage.

Bruch, H. (1978). The Golden Cage: The Enigma of Anorexia Nervosa. Cambridge, MA: Harvard University Press.

Brumberg, J. J. (1985). "Fasting girls": Reflections on writing the history of anorexia nervosa. In A. B. Smuts & J. W. Hagen (Eds.), History and research in child development. Monographs of the Society for Research in Child Development, Serial No. 211, Vol. 50 (Nos. 4-5).

Farrow, J. A. (1991). Youth alienation as an emerging pediatric health care issue. American Journal of Diseases of Children, 145, 491-494.

Haggerty, R. J. (1991). Care of the poor and underserved in America: Older adolescents: A group at special risk. American Journal of Diseases of Children, 145, 569-571.

Schinke, S. P., Botvin, G. B., & Orlandi, M. A. (1991). Substance abuse in children and adoloscents: Evaluation and intervention. Newbury Park, CA: Sage.

Seibert, J. M., & Olson, R. A. (Eds.) (1989). Children, Adolescents, and AIDS. Lincoln, NE: University of Nebraska Press.

Steinberg, L. (1989). Adolescence, 2nd edition. New York: Alfred A. Knopf.

ANSWER KEY FOR SELF-TEST ITEMS

Key Terms and Concepts

1. G. Stanley Hall
2. puberty rites
3. hypothalamus
4. pituitary
5. estrogen
6. androgens
7. human growth
8. Kurt Lewin
9. bulimia
10. larynx

Matching

1-f; 2-d; 3-g; 4-c; 5-b; 6-h; 7-a; 8-e

Multiple Choice

1. c   6. a
2. a   7. b
3. d   8. b
4. b   9. d
5. d   10. b

CHAPTER 15

COGNITIVE DEVELOPMENT DURING ADOLESCENCE

STUDY GOALS

After studying Chapter 15, you should grasp the basic issues relevant to:

1. Developments in cognition brought about by the transition to adolescence. Ways in which adolescent thought differs from that of middle childhood, and ways in which it is still unlike adult cognition.

2. The nature of intelligence. The history of efforts to define and measure intelligence, and the various theoretical views of intelligence that are held today. The relationship between IQ and sociocultural factors (e.g., economic status, ethnicity, etc.). The implications for theories of mental retardation for our understanding of intelligence and its measurement.

3. The role played by schools in adolescent development. Areas in which schools succeed and fail in the education of adolescents.

CHAPTER OVERVIEW

INTELLECTUAL DEVELOPMENT

Research on Adolescent Thought:

Keating (1980) suggests that adolescent thought differs from the child's in five ways. The adolescent:

1. can **think about abstract possibilities** without the need for concrete observations.
2. is capable of **thinking about hypotheses**, can be flexible in her thinking and consider many actual and possible solutions to a problem.
3. can **think ahead** and plan, enabling her to approach problem solving in a systematic and

efficient manner.

4. is capable of **reflective thinking**, or thinking about thinking, more efficiently (the process of thinking) and can thus develop more effective strategies for learning and solving problems. This is also called **metacognition**.

5. thinks about a **broader range of content** (e.g., politics, identity, society, existence, religion, etc.).

Piaget's Theory of Formal Operations:

In testing formal operations, Inhelder and Piaget (1958) developed a number of classic experiments to illustrate the gradual development of logic in children and their ability during the formal operations period to engage in the **scientific method of problem solving**. In contrast to the trial and error methods of middle childhood, adolescents will solve problems along a preconceived plan of action, anticipating the kinds of information necessary to solve the problem. Piaget understood the cognitive developments of this stage as a combination of brain maturation and opportunities to engage in more demanding mental tasks.

Not a Universal Stage:

Employing Piagetian tasks in cross-cultural settings, researchers have shown that while everyone attains the concrete operational stage, not everyone attains the formal operational stage. According to their findings, individuals raised in nontechnical societies and without access to schooling do not acquire the ability for formal operations. Even within our technological society not everyone achieves formal operations as measured by Piagetian tasks. However, some researchers claim that Piaget's tasks too narrowly define formalno operations by focusing solely on scientific tasks.

Individual and Sex Differences:

Accumulated knowledge is necessary to use formal operations. There are individual differences in the age at which formal operations are attained. Variations in task demands (e.g., clarifying instructions and expectations) can also change the age at which a majority of children will succeed on a given task. Sex

differences have rarely been reported in formal
operations, but when reported males have generally
performed better.

Information Processing:

Information processing theorists explain cognitive
change in terms of a better capacity to retain
information that will help them solve problems
efficiently (e.g., working memory). For example,
Scardamalia found that children could systematically work
through the problem if the demands of the task were
within their capacity for memory.

INTELLECTUAL PERFORMANCE

Another approach to the study of cognitive
development is the psychometric approach, which
emphasizes individual differences in intellectual
performance. The most common way of measuring
differences in intelligence is through standardized
intelligence tests that yield an IQ score. This score,
known as the intelligence quotient, or IQ, is the basis
for comparing a child's or adolescent's intellectual
performance with that of his same-aged peers.

What Is Intelligence?

Hebb (1972) referred to two aspects of intelligence
(A and B). **Intelligence A** refers to the individual's
innate potential to develop intellectual capacities,
while **intelligence B** refers to the level of the child's
current intellectual functioning. **Fluid intelligence**
refers to basic mental abilities such as analytic
ability, memory, and speed of thinking. **Crystallized
intelligence** refers to what the individual knows; the
individual's experience, cultural background, and
education exert an influence on crystallized intelligence
(e.g., math ability, vocabulary). Sternberg (1982) has
found that most individuals agree that intelligence
consists of three basic components: verbal intelligence
(e.g., vocabulary, verbal fluency, comprehension),
problem-solving ability (e.g., abstract thinking,
reasoning skills), and practical intelligence (ability to
identify and accomplish goals, interest in the world at
large).

Historically, psychologists have argued about how to define intelligence and the intelligent person. For example, do we consider someone who excels in all three areas of intelligence intelligent or is excelling in one area sufficient? Spearman argued that intelligence consists of two factors: a **g factor**, or general component and the **s factor**, which refers to specific abilities required for a particular task.

Measuring Intelligence:

   <u>Validity, Reliability, and Standardization</u>. Although intelligence tests differ in terms of their underlying conceptualization of intelligence, a common set of principles guides the construction of such tests. First, the test must have **validity**, or it must measure what it proposes to measure. In fact, IQ tests tend to predict academic performance. Second, the test must be **reliable**, yielding the same results when we retest an individual over a short period of time. Finally, tests must be **standardized**, which refers to the establishment of standard items, procedures, and norms. Two important principles of standardization must be emphasized:

   1. The larger the groups of children used to standardize the test, the more applicable the test will be to other children of similar circumstances; and
   2. The standardization sample must correspond to the characteristics of the total population of children we wish to test (e.g., SES, regions of the country, sex composition).

   Binet and Simon, working in France, constructed a test consisting of 30 items presented in ascending order of difficulty. They lengthened the test to include different tasks for each different age group. This allowed Simon and Binet to determine the child's **mental age** (MA) which referred to the age typically associated with the problems the child could solve. Thus, a very bright child who chronologically was 5 years old might have an MA of 7. However, it is difficult to compare a 5-year-old with an MA of 7 and a nine-year-old with an MA of 11. To compare children of different ages, the concept of the intelligence quotient, which remains relatively stable with age, was derived based on Stern's 1911 formula: IQ = (Mental Age (MA)/Chronological Age (CA)) *

100. We now use more sophisticated statistical methods to calculate IQ scores.

Lewis Terman revised the test developed by Binet and Simon and standardized it for use with American children. The test was called the Stanfo-Binet. Several other IQ tests were developed by David Wechsler. All of them yield a verbal IQ score, a **performance IQ** score, and a total or **Full Scale** IQ score.

What Do IQ Tests Measure?

An IQ test may not predict how well an individual adapts to life circumstances (e.g., managing money, holding a job, interacting with peers). In addition, while IQ scores (especially the verbal IQ) are strong predictors of academic success, many other factors such as motivation and comfort in the testing setting influence intellectual performance. In addition, **cognitive style**, for example the tendency to respond in a hurried manner -- **an impulsive style** -- or slowly and deliberately -- **a reflective style**, may also influence performance on IQ tests. Finally many critics of IQ tests argue that the tests are culturally biased and thereby give an unfair advantage to middle-class, white children. Indeed, students from minority groups and lower socioeconomic levels tend to score low on such tests; therefore the educational system is more likely to label them slow learners or mentally retarded and place them in slow-paced educational programs or in special education classes. Due to concerns about these biases, California banned the use of IQ test scores as a major basis for placement in special education. The courts now require schools to use several criteria, including practical intelligence, or the child's ability to adapt to life circumstances. It has not been possible to develop a perfectly culture-fair test and it is likely that once developed, the test would not predict school achievement, inasmuch as successful school performance is also culturally biased.

The Adolescent in School:

The education provided to adolescents must accommodate the more sophisticated level of cognitive functioning. In addition to broadening the content, we expect adolescents to cover topics in more depth and to make use of hypotheses and abstract reasoning. Not all teachers provide the kind of educational experiences that enable students to attain formal operational thought because some will continue to emphasize rote learning rather than active problem solving. Additionally, not all students pursue the same academic course. Many schools have a system of tracking students into high-achieving, middle- and low-track classes. Many have criticized this system, arguing that the slow-track students will regard themselves as failures and both slow- and middle-track students will be denied opportunities which might facilitate growth and positive self-regard. It is critical that test scores and scholastic performance be evaluated to provide rather than to deny appropriate educational opportunities.

Discussion of Social Issues: High School Compensatory Education:

The primary focus of school intervention efforts has been in the early childhood years. This policy stems from the concept of the **critical period** of intervention, that unless we identify and ameliorate learning difficulties at an early age, students are foredoomed to educational failure. Thus, we leave unexplored possibilities for intervening in adolescence. Fuerstein (1980) worked with low-IQ youngsters (IQ of 60 to 80, which would place some in the mentally retarded range). His strategy is **mediated learning experiences**, which involves guiding the interactions of youngsters in their interactions with the environment so that the youngsters can gradually adapt to new ways of perceiving the world and processing information.

Illiteracy in the United States:

Many high school students either drop out of school without ever acquiring basic reading and writing skills or graduate from high school without attaining them. As a result, these young people are functionally illiterate (cannot write a check, address an envelope). Approximately 17 to 21 million English-speaking Americans are functionally illiterate.

National attention on illiterate high school graduates has resulted in highly publicized lawsuits in which individuals have sued school systems for failing to provide an adequate education. Some states now require seniors to demonstrate an adequate grasp of basic skills before they can graduate. Other states have passed laws abolishing "social promotions": students below their grade level passing into the next grade. However, the value of these measures is questionable as they do not address the basic issue of decreasing illiteracy.

Preventing Truancy and School Dropout:

Illiteracy stems from a number of problems. One is that many children do not attend school. Over 3 million children between the ages of 7 and 17 do not attend school and 1 million are between ages 7 and 15. Truant children are likely to be poor, nonwhite, and non-English speaking. Forty-five percent of Hispanic youths never complete high school. The societal costs of truancy and school dropouts are enormous. The unemployment rates of school dropouts is more than twice that of high school graduates. Students who are at risk for dropping out can be identified as early as the seventh grade; they are generally highly aggressive in their behavior, are often absent, may be living in stressful family situations, feel anxiety because of economic need, do not do well in school, and often face intense personal problems unrelated to the school experience. Responding to these students' needs in order to alleviate some of the pressures they are experiencing and to make learning experiences relevant for them may be more effective than assuming a punitive or criminal stance toward truancy. While punitive approaches are understandable, they tend to lead to further rebellion and eventually school drop-out.

Do Schools Make a Difference?

Several schools have been effective not only in reducing truancy and dropout rates but also in increasing student achievement. Effective schools have encouraged parental involvement and tend to assign homework on a regular basis. In a study of individual differences in academic achievement among low-income adolescents in England, Rutter noted the following characteristics in the schools that fostered good behavior:

1. These schools placed an emphasis on academics

190

and assigned homework and similar activities;
2. Teachers in successful schools spent more time interacting with the class as a whole than with individual students;
3. Students enjoyed favorable conditions at school (e.g., free use of the facility, access to telephones);
4. Students had the opportunity to assume responsibility and participate in a variety of activities;
5. There was continuity in the school population in terms of teachers and students.

In a similar study of secondary schools in large American urban areas, successful schools (80 percent of students graduated) emphasized student achievement and required all students to complete a basic curriculum. The less effective schools did not place any burden on the students but let them define their own roles and curriculum. Schools that set high expectations for success and give students opportunities to achieve are more likely than other schools to have successful students.

KEY TERMS AND CONCEPTS

Fill in the blanks with the best word or phrase. Check your answers against the answer key at the end of this chapter.

1. Thinking about thinking is called _____.

2. The Piagetian stage reached during adolesence is _____.

3. _____ divides groups of students according to their academic performance and dictates different academic courses of study for them.

4. Hebb's "intelligence ____" refers to the child's innate potential to develop intellectual capacities.

5. Spearman's _____ represented the general intellectual ability relevant to all intellectual tasks.

6. The _____ of a test refers to the consistency of the results obtained upon different testings of the same individuals.

7. A test's degree of _____ indicates how successfully it measures what it is intended to measure.

8. The IQ test measures intellectual _____.

9. The adolescent's belief that no one can experience emotions and events as he or she does is an example of adolescent _____.

10. Approximately 70% of all mental retardation is _____ retardation with no known organic cause.

MATCHING

1.	Sternberg	a.	mediated learning experiences
2.	Hebb	b.	personal fable
3.	Howard Gardner	c.	first standardized test
4.	Spearman	d.	IQ scores and placement
5.	Binet	e.	U.S. version of Binet
6.	Feuerstein	f.	g factor
7.	Peter W. Doe	g.	3 components of intelligence
8.	Larry P.	h.	intelligence A and B
9.	Terman	i.	7 kinds of intelligence
10.	David Elkind	j.	adequate education

MULTIPLE CHOICE SELF-TEST

_____ 1. _____ described intelligence as having 2 components: a "g factor," or general intelligence, and the "s factor," representative of special intelligences for particular tasks.
   a. Terman
   b. Binet
   c. Hebb
   d. Spearman

_____ 2. The formal operations period emerges at about age
   a. 5
   b. 7
   c. 12
   d. 17

_____3. Hebb called the intelligence that referred to level of intellectual functioning
   a. intelligence A
   b. intelligence B
   c. fluid intelligence
   d. crystallized intelligence

_____4. The extent to which a test measures what it is supposed to measure is called its
   a. reliability
   b. standardization
   c. accuracy
   d. validity

_____5. According to Stern's formulation, an 8-year-old who functions at a 4-year-old level has an IQ of
   a. 4
   b. 8
   c. 4/8 X 100
   c. 8/4 X 100

_____6. IQ scores and school achievement have
   a. a negative correlation
   b. almost no correlation, only about .03
   c. a correlation of about .60
   d. a perfect correlation, or 1.00

_____7. Feuerstein is known for his research on
   a. low-IQ adolescents
   b. the development of thinking about science
   c. the components of IQ
   d. fluid and crystallized IQ

_____8. _____ of all people fall into the "normal" IQ range.
   a. 10%
   b. 50%
   c. one-third
   d. two-thirds

_____9. Lewis Terman took Binet's IQ test and
   a.   denounced it as culturally biased and unfair
   b.   adapted it for use in the U.S.
   c.   performed its first standardization
   d.   translated it into French

_____10. The case of <u>Peter W. Doe v. The San Francisco</u>
        <u>Unified School District</u> was about
   a.   the use of IQ scores in educational placement
   b.   the school's responsibility to provide adequate
        education
   c.   the legality of "tracking"
   d.   the use of culturally biased IQ tests

RECOMMENDATIONS FOR FURTHER READING

Inhelder, B., & Piaget, J. (1985). The Growth of Logical Thinking From Childhood to Adolescence. New York: Basic Books.

Keating, D.P. (1980). Thinking Processes in Adolescence. In J. Adelson (Ed.), Handbook of Adolescent Psychology. New York: Wiley.

Overton, W.F., & Meehan, A.M. (1982). Individual differences in formal operational thought: Sex role and learned helplessness. Child Development, 53, 1536-1543.

Rutter, M. (1979). Fifteen Thousand Hours: Secondary Schools and Their Effect on Children. Cambridge, MA: Harvard University Press.

Scarr, S. (1981). Race, Social Class, and Individual Differences in I.Q. Hillsdale, NJ: Lawrence Erlbaum Associates.

ANSWER KEY FOR SELF-TEST ITEMS

Key Terms and Concepts

1. metacognition
2. formal operations
3. tracking
4. A
5. g factor
6. reliability
7. validity
8. performance
9. egocentrism
10. cultural familial

Matching

1-g; 2-h; 3-i; 4-f; 5-c; 6-a; 7-j; 8-d; 9-e;
10-b

Multiple Choice Self-Test

1.	d	6.	c
2.	c	7.	a
3.	b	8.	d
4.	d	9.	b
5.	c	10.	b

CHAPTER 16

SOCIAL AND EMOTIONAL DEVELOPMENT DURING ADOLESCENCE

STUDY GOALS

A careful study of Chapter 16 should help you to understand:

1. The social and emotional aspects of adolescence and adolescent development, including developments related to self-concept, peer relations, and relationships within the context of family and school.

2. Social issues affecting adolescents, including runaway youth, homelessness, and juvenile delinquency.

3. Historical changes in social development, vocational identity, and employment. The impact of local and national economic crises on youth development.

CHAPTER OVERVIEW

THE SEARCH FOR A PERSONAL IDENTITY

The task of defining oneself in adolescence may be very difficult because there are many possibilities and the adolescent is in a transitional phase.

Theoretical Perspectives:

The Psychosocial Theory of Erik Erikson. Erikson (1963, 1968) has had an extensive influence on current views of adolescent development. According to Erikson, the central crisis facing the adolescent is **identity versus role confusion**. Throughout childhood, the individual gradually develops some sense of him or herself as a unique being. Facilitated by newly acquired cognitive skills (e.g., abstract reasoning) and interpersonal awareness the adolescent thinks about who he is and who he will become.

Crisis and Commitment. While our personal identity is not completely formed during adolescence, Erikson emphasizes that many decisions made during this phase of development have important implications for how we deal with our young adulthood, middle age, and old age. He further points out that the task of forming a personal identity is difficult. **Identity achievement** refers to a commitment to decisions about oneself and one's future. In contrast, role confusion refers to anxiety and confusion which is related to an inability to make decisions and choices regarding personal roles.

    <u>Contemporary Viewpoints</u>. Marcia (1966, 1980, 1988), building on Erikson's work, interviewed college students about their occupational choice, religion, and political beliefs. Marcia noted that identity formation is a gradual process that involves four modes of resolution:

    1) **Identity Diffusion** - a failure to experience an increasing cohesion of identity; some adolescents withdraw from efforts to shape their identity or feel ambivalent about decisions;
    2) **Foreclosure** - premature identity formation occurs when adolescents fail to question incorporated family and societal values;
    3) **Moratorium** - a postponement of a resolution. This can be constructive when it affords the opportunity to evaluate a broader array of options or destructive if the postponement persists well into adulthood; and
    4) **Identity Achievement** - finding an identity and making commitments and choices consistent with beliefs and desires.

    Waterman (1985) notes that we may achieve identity in one domain earlier than in others (e.g., career or political beliefs).

The Social Context:

    Ease of identity achievement is in part a function of the societal context. In primitive cultures the transition to adulthood often involves a test of skills or bravery. In such societies there may be few available roles to choose from as the society is relatively stable over multiple generations. In complex societies such as our own, the individual must synthesize various identifications and choose from a wide variety of roles. These decisions must be made in the context of one's own talents and capabilities and the feasibility of pursuing specific options. Society will also set limits on options available to the individual based on culturally held prejudices (e.g., race, sex, social class).

Vocational Identity. A job is one way we define our place in society and the kinds of people we associate with. In high school adolescents decide to pursue either an academic course of study that will lead to college or a vocational course. Only half of middle-class adolescents and one-quarter of black adolescents attend college. A majority of adolescents work more than 16 hours a week while attending school. Working is positive in that it provides the opportunity to learn about work options and acquire specific work-related skills. However, it may be negative in that it takes time away from school-related activities. Indeed, adolescents who are working more than 14 hours a week tend to maintain a lower grade point average than adolescents who are not working or working fewer hours.

Youth Unemployment. Although part-time employment is available for high-school students, youth who seek full-time employment have a great deal of difficulty finding jobs. This is especially true for black and Hispanic youths. Economic conditions and shifts in the labor market contribute to high rates of unemployment among teens. The current economy seeks literate, technically trained and committed workers but many students drop out of high school or complete high school functionally illiterate and with few if any technical skills. Furthermore, the implementation of a higher minimum wage limited options for teen employment. Educational and training programs designed to increase teen employment have demonstrated that their benefits far outweigh the costs.

The Depression Era. In highlighting the role of social context on identity formation, Glen Elder (1980) gives an example of adolescents who grew up in the 1920s and 1930s. During these years there was a social revolution marked by the liberalization of social norms (e.g., women's roles were expanded with increased education and career options). The Depression of the 1930s followed this prosperous period. The Oakland Growth Study, begun in 1930, was a longitudinal study conducted by the Berkeley Institute of Human Development. As a result of the Depression, many young women who

199

planned to pursue an education and career had to assume more traditional roles within their family as homemakers. Boys and girls who lived through the Depression were family-centered and considered children to be the most important aspect of a marriage. They emphasized the responsibilities of parenthood and stressed the value of dependability in children.

Currently, unemployed teens have a sense of hopelessness about their future and some of them resort to crime. Another trend noted among teens is that in contrast to the rebellion and social consciousness typical of adolescents in the 1960s and 1970s, teens in the 1980s were becoming increasingly conservative.

Sex Roles and Sexual Behavior:

The economy is only one aspect of society which influences identity formation. Our society has also witnessed a sexual revolution that has many consequences for sex roles and sexual behavior. These changes have had the greatest impact on girls as they are deferring marriage and parenthood while they pursue careers.

Another obvious effect of the sexual revolution is the increase in sexual activity among adolescents. One half of the one million teenage girls in the U.S. who become pregnant will carry their pregnancies to term. The vast majority of these teen mothers are single and choosing to raise their babies. Teenage mothers and their infants are often living in conditions of poverty and do not receive adequate health care. In addition, parenthood has a devastating effect on the mother's education. They are much less likely to finish high school. Fortunately, young people can redefine their identities even after they are off to a difficult start. Many teenage mothers have benefitted from support programs which enable them to complete their education while quality child care is provided to their children.

Peers:

The choice of friends is one of the major factors in the search for identity. Friends are critical in the determination of one's life-style and values and provide emotional support during a time of social transition.

<u>Friendships</u>. While friends are important from early childhood through old age, Berndt and Perry (1990) described the distinctive features of friendships during adolescence:

1. Loyalty and faithfulness are important characteristics of a friend.
2. Competition with close friends is avoided, aiming instead for equality through sharing.
3. Adolescents have more intimate friends than younger children, viewing friendships as emotionally supportive relationships.

Girls are more likely to talk about the importance of intimacy in friendships than are boys. Boys tend to lag behind girls in terms of changes in the quality of their friendships. In addition, some investigators report that girls value friendships more than boys. Other researchers have not found these differences. A sex difference in friendships is consistent with theorists who argue that society has stronger interpersonal expectations for girls and a higher emphasis on skills, achievement, and self-sufficiency for boys. By late adolescence physical maturation is complete, and adolescents are typically more at ease with themselves and have developed a more secure sense of their identity. Thus, friendships tend to be more relaxed. In late adolescence **individuality** in friends is valued.

<u>Cliques and Crowds</u>. Friendships exist within the larger social structure of peer relationships. Peer groups of 5 to 20 members which are closed to outsiders and based on shared interests and values are typical in adolescence. Dunphy conducted a study of adolescent peer groups in Australia in the 1960s. He found that in early adolescence, these groups are same-age, single-sex **cliques** of approximately five members who share similar backgrounds. By approximately age 14, boys and girls in separate cliques tend to interact. Gradually the cliques merge, and by mid- to late adolescence teens spend most of their time in a **crowd** that can include as many as 20 members of both sexes. Eventually, in early adulthood, individuals prefer to congregate in groups of couples rather than in a crowd. A more recent study of American high school students revealed membership in one of five major cliques: the jocks or athletes, the populars, the

normals, the druggies, and the nobodies.

Popularity and Rejection. Within cliques and crowds there are typically a few individuals who stand out as leaders and who are considered the most popular members. Popular children are more likely to be friendly, cheerful, humorous, and capable of initiating activities for the whole group. Similarly, there are adolescents who are considered socially awkward or unattractive. Researchers distinguish between **neglected adolescents**, who do not have friends but are not disliked, and **rejected adolescents**, who are more likely to be disliked, disruptive, and aggressive. Neglected adolescents typically have low self-esteem and are afraid to approach peers because they fear rejection.

Conformity. The need to conform during adolescence is related to age and status in the peer group. Early adolescence is characterized by a dramatic increase in the demand to conform, which peaks between ages 11 to 13. Over the course of adolescence there is a decrease in the need to conform. Further, adolescents do not depend solely on peers. While seeking out peers for choices regarding clothing and music, they tend to seek their parents' advice regarding issues such as employment and choice of college.

The Family:

Most adolescents believe that their parents are supportive of them. Adolescents most often choose occupational paths, friends, and political values that are consistent with their parents' aspirations for them and they tend to maintain a close attachment to their parents.

Changes in Family Interactions. In attempting to establish their own identity, adolescents may question their parents' values and beliefs. Early in adolescence conflicts occur in connection with household responsibilities and appropriateness of dress. In later adolescence disagreements are more likely to involve dating and drug and alcohol use. In general, conflict is greatest when adolescents are undergoing dramatic physical change. Parents and teens must adapt to the 'new' stature, 'new' reproductive capability, and 'new' cognitive competence of the adolescent. In addition, the cost of maintaining an adolescent, which is approximately 140 percent that of a younger child, can be quite stressful. The task of parenting an adolescent is quite different from the task of parenting a younger child. It involves providing support and encouragement while nurturing the adolescent's quest for independence. Parents may be contemplating their own past and future and redefining their existence following their child's departure. The failure to adjust to these many changes and developments may lead to significant family disruption.

Parenting Styles. Diana Baumrind, who studied parenting styles and their effects on preschoolers, also reviewed the literature on parent-adolescent relationships. She found that while the adolescent brought his own temperament and personality to the relationship, the parents' child-rearing approaches and reactions have a definite influence on the child's personality and behavior. Baumrind describes three parenting styles:

Authoritative parents - show interest in activities and are warm and supportive in interactions. They provide standards and autonomy in a flexible manner which accepts the child's perspective. Teens whose parents are authoritative are more likely to be socially active and responsible, have high self-esteem, and commit themselves to values and goals following self-evaluation.

Authoritarian parents - are controlling in their interactions with the adolescent. They expect compliance from their adolescents and are unwilling to adjust to the adolescent's need for independence leading to more conflictual interactions. Teens of authoritarian parents have difficulty developing their own identity and are less likely to engage in self-evaluation.

Permissive parents - are undemanding of their adolescents. They expect their adolescents to be sufficiently mature to make decisions independently and provide few or inconsistent rules, standards, or expectations. Permissive parents may interact more like peers than authority figures. This lack of direction may lead to teens feeling confused and rejected.

        Adolescent Abuse. Physical and emotional abuse of
adolescents is prevalent and related to inappropriate
parenting behaviors. Because adolescents can strike
back, dangerous domestic quarrels, involving mutual
assault, sometimes result from teen abuse. Garbarino
(1986) notes the following characteristics of families in
which abuse of adolescents is more likely to occur:

1. the family contains a stepparent;
2. the adolescents are less socially competent or
   developmentally delayed;
3. the family is troubled by divorce;
4. the parents are authoritarian.

Discussion of Social Issues: Runaway, Homeless, and
Delinquent Young People:

        Adolescents subjected to abuse sometimes run away
from home and then must contend with homelessness. Ill-
equipped to obtain their own in the world, many adopt a
life of delinquency and/or prostitution.

        Runaways. About 500,000 youths run away from home
each year. Some are seduced into a life of prostitution
by pimps and hustlers who then torture them physically
and emotionally. According to Artenstein (1990), 36
percent of runaways are fleeing from sexual or physical
abuse and 44 percent are running from other severe
problems in the family. Only 50 percent of runaways have
the option to return to the family or be placed in foster
care. In 25 percent of cases, youths remain homeless and
have to live on the street.

        Homeless Youths. Homeless youths are rejected by
their families. Sometimes these families are
overburdened with financial responsibilities. Sometimes
a parent's lover subjects the adolescent to physical or
sexual abuse and the adolescent leaves knowing they are
not welcome to return. There are also adolescents who
are members of homeless families. Numerous federally and
state-funded programs are available in cities across the
nation to help runaway and homeless youth. For example,
the National Runaway Switchboard helps teens get in touch
with their parents in the hope that the youngsters can go
home. Youth shelters provide temporary respite from life
on the street.

Delinquent Youths. The number of juveniles in
custody in increasing. Delinquency refers to a pattern
of destructive behavior, including murder, assault,
vandalism, and theft, as well as truancy, promiscuity, and
running away from home. Fifty-four percent of serious
crimes such as murder, assault, and robbery are committed
by youths age 13 to 18; 31 percent of all general arrests
nationally involve individuals age 18 and under.
Delinquent youths typically have low self-esteem, a
history of school problems, lower IQ than average for the
general population, and a history of abuse and neglect.
The drug trade has contributed to violence among young
people and to a nationwide spread of youth gangs.

Facilitating the Transition from Childhood to Adulthood:

     Experts estimate that 7 million, or one in four
adolescents, are at high risk for multiple behavior
problems and school failure and that another 7 million
are at moderate risk. Some experts recommend that
prevention efforts based in the schools should be used as
the primary means for addressing the needs of youths.
For example, the Carnegie Council on Adolescent
Development (1989) notes that:

     1. Schools need to become small communities for
     learning where stable, close, and mutually respectful
     relationships can develop;
     2. Schools must be staffed with teachers trained in
     adolescence; and
     3. Schools must provide health services to teens.

     In addition, to bridge the gap between school and
work students should have the opportunity to participate
in internships, apprenticeships and preemployment
training for specific jobs. Finally, in addition to the
focus on the needs of adolescents is the importance of
focusing on the needs of families.

KEY TERMS AND CONCEPTS

Complete each item with the best word or phrase. Check
your answers against those at the chapter's end.

1. For Erikson, the psychosocial crisis of adolescence
is _____.

2. Successful resolution of the adolescent quest to
identify with a particular role or set of roles results
in _____.

3. _____ may result when the adolescent is
unprepared to deal with a multiplicity of choices and
opportunities.

4. Premature identity formation, or _____,
occurs when the adolescent accepts the values of parents
or society without adequately examining and questioning
them.

5. An adolescent who postpones college in order to "find
herself" is observing a period of _____.

6. _____ is the substance most widely abused
by teens.

7. Elder's examination of the effect of the Great
Depression on teens used data from the
_____.

8. The effect of _____
has been to price teens out of the job market to a great
extent.

9. A 1978 program allowing employers to write off 85% of
the salary paid to teens proved to be an
effective/ineffective way to boost youth employment.

10. Dunphy's classic 1963 study focused on the nature
and development of _____.

MULTIPLE CHOICE SELF-TEST

_____ 1. The members of most cliques in early
         adolescence are
      a. all girls
      b. all boys
      c. all of the same sex
      d. of different sexes

_____ 2. Teens who are not necessarily disliked by peers
         but who nonetheless have no friends are
      a. neglected adolescents
      b. engaging in moratorium behavior
      c. foreclosed
      d. rejected adolescents

_____ 3. The need to conform peaks at about age
      a. 5
      b. 7
      c. 12
      d. 16

_____ 4. For advice about life-course decisions, teens
         tend to consult
      a. peers
      b. teachers
      c. ministers and professional counselors
      d. parents

_____ 5. Following the Depression of the 1930s,
      a. women assumed more traditionally feminine roles
      b. women assumed more powerful roles in the family
      c. most women left their husbands
      d. most women immediately sought marriage and a
         family

_____ 6. _____ parents are controlling in
         their interactions with their teenage children.
      a. authoritative
      b. authoritarian
      c. permissive
      d. divorcing

_____7. Close to _____ of all cases of child
abuse involve maltreatment of adolescents.
a. 10%
b. one third
c. one half
d. 90%

_____8. Which of these was not a family characteristic
associated with increased risk of adolescent
maltreatment, according to Garbarino?
a. divorce is a feature of the family profile
b. a stepparent is more likely to be in the family
c. the parents are authoritarian
d. both parents work outside the home

_____9. The rate of juvenile delinquency is
a. increasing
b. decreasing
c. increasing, but only for white females
d. increasing, but only for black females

_____10. The William T. Grant Foundation Commission on
Work, Family, and Citizenship recommends
a. that all youth should attend college
b. that teens be adequately prepared for
employment
c. school segregation based on race
d. school segregation based on aptitude

RECOMMENDATIONS FOR FURTHER READING

Adams, G. R., Gullotta, T. P., & Montemayor, R. (1992).
Adolescent Identity Formation. Newbury Park, CA: Sage.

Hurrelmann, K., & Engel, W. (Eds.) (1989). The social
world of adolescents: International perspectives.
Berlin: Walter de Gruyter.

Kroger, J. (1989). Identity in Adolescence: Balance
Between Self and Other. New York: Routledge.

Stiffman, A. R., & Davis, L. E. (1990). Ethnic Issues in
Adolescent Mental Health. Newbury Park, CA: Sage.

Turnbull, C. (1984). The Human Cycle. London: Jonathan Cape.

ANSWER KEY

Key Terms and Concepts

1. identity vs. role confusion
2. identity achievement
3. role diffusion
4. foreclosure
5. moratorium
6. alcohol
7. Oakland Growth Study
8. federal minimum wage laws
9. ineffective
10. cliques

Multiple Choice

1. c
2. a
3. c
4. d
5. b

6. b
7. c
8. d
9. a
10. b